GOD SEEKERS
for a NEW AGE

THEMES FOR TODAY
James O'Gara, General Editor

ROCH A.
KERESZTY

GOD SEEKERS
for a NEW AGE

From Crisis Theology to "Christian Atheism"

PFLAUM PRESS, DAYTON, OHIO

1970

Library of Congress Catalog Card Number: 76-93005
Printed in the United States of America

CONTENTS

ACKNOWLEDGMENTS

The author wishes to thank the following for the use of copyrighted material:

From *The Death of God Debate*, edited by Jackson Lee Ice and John J. Carey. Copyright © MCMLXVII, The Westminster Press. Used by permission.

From *Honest to God*, by John A. T. Robinson. Published in the U. S. A., 1963, by The Westminster Press, Philadelphia. © SCM Press, Ltd., London, 1963. Used by permission.

Thomas J. J. Altizer for extracts from *Oriental Mysticism and Biblical Eschatology*.

From *Theological Explorations* by Paul van Buren, reprinted with permission of The Macmillan Company. Copyright © Paul van Buren, 1965, 1968.

From *Letters and Papers from Prison* by Dietrich Bonhoeffer, reprinted with permission of The Macmillan Company. Copyright by The Macmillan Company, 1953. © SCM Press, Ltd., 1967.

From *The Secular Meaning of the Gospel* by Paul van Buren, reprinted with permission of The Macmillan Company. © Paul van Buren, 1963.

Association Press of New York for extracts from *The New Essence of Christianity* by William Hamilton.

Robert Kimball and the University of Chicago Press for extracts from *Systematic Theology* by Paul Tillich, Volumes I and III.

Journal of Ecumenical Studies for extracts from "A Translation of Tillich's Idea of God" which appeared in the Winter, 1967 (Vol. IV, No. 4) issue.

From *Radical Theology and the Death of God,* copyright © 1966 by Thomas J. J. Altizer and William Hamilton, reprinted by permission of the publishers, The Bobbs-Merrill Company, Inc.

Commonweal for extracts from the statement by Father Adolf in the March 15, 1968, issue.

John Knox Press for extracts from "The Shape of a Radical Theology" by William Hamilton and "Theology in the Context of Culture" by Paul van Buren in *Frontline Theology,* edited by Dean Peerman.

GOD SEEKERS
for a NEW AGE

INTRODUCTION

Today, the death-of-God fad is dead. Its demise came earlier than most theologians and the general public had anticipated.

The death-of-God received its first contemporary formulation in 1960 when William Hamilton, at that time a moderate Baptist theologian of the neoorthodox school, declared at the National Interseminary Movement Conference in Denver: "The great new fact of our time is the disappearance of God from the world. Our theology must be the theology of the death of God."[1] At that time, few people bothered to listen. Even Hamilton's book, *The New Essence of Christianity* (1961), and van Buren's *The Secular Meaning of the Gospel* (1963) went largely unnoticed. Only in 1964, after the *Honest-to-God* debate had quieted down, did the fact of a new trend within American Protestantism become increasingly evident. During the second half of 1965 and the first months of 1966, *The New Yorker, The New York Times,* and *Time* turned this current theology into a public affair. Three "younger theologians" achieved national fame via the movement: Thomas J. J. Altizer, William Hamilton, and Paul M. van Buren. Passionate discussions before television cameras and sensation-hungry reporters followed Altizer and Hamilton as they moved from campus to campus. For a while, it seemed as though they

---

[1] Quoted by J. Robert Nelson, "Deicide, Theothanasia, Or What Do You Mean?" *The Meaning of the Death of God,* ed. by B. Murchland (New York: Random, Vintage Books, 1967), p. 194.

3

would inaugurate a powerful "religious" movement with a definite confession of faith (the death of God), a program of apostolic action (to proclaim the gospel of the death of God), and a strange kind of mysticism (to celebrate the death of God). Some students shuddered with emotion, and their eyes were filled with tears, wrote the *National Observer*, as the choir at North Carolina Wesleyan College sang a Requiem in honor of the deceased God: "Your God is dead . . . He died in the darkness of your image. He died because you held his hand too tightly. . . ."[2]

By 1967, the first shock had subsided. This was the year when responses to the death-of-God were collected and published,[3] when Altizer tried to establish his theological ancestry by pointing to a radical tradition within Christianity which culminated in his vision of Christian atheism.[4] Yet it was already evident that the death-of-God theologians had failed to establish a major school or religious movement. No other theologian joined them, and within the "trio" itself basic and insurmountable differences arose.[5] Even theologians who had at first sympathized with them dismissed their conclusions: ". . . that is not what we meant."[6]

Why, then, write a book today about Christian atheism when everybody seems to have forgotten it, when even Hamilton, Altizer, and van Buren have become quite reticent? I feel the death-of-God phenomenon is still very much with us, not as an openly declared theological position, but as a clearly perceptible mood, a powerful undercurrent which deeply influences Chris-

---

[2]*National Observer*, January 1, 1966.

[3]See the books in the "Selected Bibliography" listed under II/B.

[4]See Thomas J. J. Altizer, *Toward a New Christianity: Readings in the Death of God Theology* (New York: Harcourt, Brace & World, 1967).

[5]"Langdon Gilkey says we belong to a 'God is dead' movement, but I think Altizer and Bill Hamilton and I are saying different things." Van Buren made this remark in an interview with Ved Mehta, "The New Theologian. I. Ecce Homo," *The New Yorker*, November 13, 1965, p. 144.

[6]Martin E. Marty and Dean G. Peerman, "The Turn from Mere Anarchy," *New Theology*, No. 3 (New York: Macmillan, 1966), p. 13.

tian thinking and living. In my opinion this phenomenon is at least as strong in American Catholicism as in other Christian churches, if not stronger. I wish to make it clear, however, that I by no means share the fanatic pessimism of *Triumph* magazine in regard to Catholicism's present turmoil. There are many promising signs of a genuine theological and spiritual renewal, but as Church history shows, authentic reform and development are always threatened by accompanying tendencies which constitute a mortal danger for the authenticity of the renewal. It is in this qualified sense that I speak about a death-of-God mood in the Catholic Church. For there are some particular symptoms which reveal the presence of this mood.

At a certain popular level of theologizing there is an increasing tendency to consider man as *the* object of faith. A revealing example of such man-centeredness is the new "creed" of Father Robert Adolfs who cautiously avoids even mentioning the word "God":

I believe in man
and in a world in which
it is good to live for all mankind;
and that it is our task
to create such a world . . .
. . . I believe in Jesus of Nazareth,
and I want to orientate my life to him.
In doing so, I believe that I
am drawn into the mysterious relationship
with the one whom he called his Father . . .
And I believe in the resurrection,
whatever it may mean.
Amen.[7]

Another area of Church life where genuine and false reform

[7]From a response by Robert Adolfs to the Symposium "Troubled Priest," *Commonweal,* March 15, 1968, pp. 714-715. R. Adolfs is prior of the Augustinian Priory of Marienhage in Holland. His book *The Grave of God* has greatly influenced a certain segment of the American Catholic intelligentsia.

develop side by side is the liturgy. The main distortion here is to consider liturgy *exclusively* as a means to form a human community and make this community sensitive to the needs of mankind. In this perspective the God-centered dimension of liturgy as worship of the Father in union with Christ and each other has been forgotten.[8]

A look at many of today's religion textbooks confirms the impression that man has become the center of religion. God serves as a means to help achieve freedom, happiness, personal fulfillment.[9] I cannot help being convinced, therefore, from the representative examples cited that to dismiss the death-of-God issue as an outmoded fad is to repress a problem we would not like to face.

From a distance of about three years, I hope we can analyze more objectively the development of Christian atheism, perceive at least some of the causes which engendered it, and discuss the problems it raised. After a short evaluation of Bishop Robinson's *Honest to God*, an ambiguous introductory phase of the death-of-God controversy (chapter I), I will attempt to analyze the thought of the three "hard radicals," W. Hamilton, T. Altizer, and P. van Buren (chapters II, III, and IV). Their bizarre and sometimes shockingly inconsistent theology can be understood only against their theological background. Thus in chapters V, VI, VII, and VIII, I will examine the contributions of crisis theology and neoorthodoxy to their thought, in particu-

---

[8] Indeed the liturgy is the worship of the community, and the central liturgical act, the Eucharist, builds up the assembly of the faithful as the one body of Christ responsible before God for the life of the whole world. But all this takes place because the Eucharist unites us through Christ to the Father in thanksgiving and adoration.

[9] Again, I would like to stress that all this is a tendency, and not an explicit position. Besides, we should gratefully acknowledge many values in the lively and "relevant" presentation of textbooks like *The Roots of Faith, Book 4. Man Comes of Age* (New York: Harcourt, Brace & World, 1968), and Andrew Panzarella, *Growth in Christ. Life and Light Series* (New York: Sadlier, 1968).

lar the influence of Bultmann, Tillich, Barth, and Bonhoeffer.[10] Only after this investigation can one attempt to draw "the lesson" of Christian atheism and point out the direction in which more fruitful research can be made.

Roch A. Kereszty, S.O. Cist.

[10]"Crisis theology" can be used as a general category to describe the early position of Bultmann, Tillich, Barth, and Bonhoeffer. All four insist that sinful man stands under the condemning and saving judgment (*krisis* in Greek) of God's Word. Later, each of the four developed in a different direction. The later Barth and Bonhoeffer are usually classified as "neo-orthodox" theologians. In the present volume, I will not treat the whole historical background of "the death of God." What concerns me here are the immediate theological roots. For its beginnings in Lutheranism, Hegel, and Nietzsche, see Martin E. Marty, "Whenever God Dies: Protestant Roots of the Problem of God," *Speaking of God,* ed. by Denis Dirscherl (Milwaukee: Bruce, 1967), pp. 74-93; W. Richard Comstock, "Theology after the 'Death of God,' " in *The Meaning of the Death of God,* pp. 212-265.

PRELUDE

1

THE HONEST TO GOD DEBATE

The title of the French edition of *Honest to God*, "God without God," sums up ingeniously the paradoxical and even contradictory character of Bishop J. A. T. Robinson's theological best-seller.[1] He seems to be "at a sort of halfway point between an honest-to-God atheism and an honest-to-God theism."[2] As the Bishop himself acknowledges (p. 8), there is a dividing line "running through the middle of himself," between the Christian and the secular humanist. His intention is clearly and genuinely religious:[3] "I want God to be as real for our modern, secular, scientific world as he ever was for the 'ages of faith.' "[4] He has inspiring religious insights. Neverthe-

---

[1]London: SCM Press, 1963; Philadelphia: Westminster Press, 1963. Unless otherwise noted, all page references incorporated within the text are to *Honest to God*.

[2]Albert C. Outler, Schubert M. Ogden, John Deschner, *Trialogue on "The Death of God"* (Dallas, Texas: Perkins School of Theology, TM Publications, 1966), p. 10. Here Outler applies the expression not to *Honest to God*, but to the general climate in today's liberal Protestant theology.

[3]Here I use the word *religious* in a general, more or less Tillichian sense, which Robinson is also prepared to accept, although in his book he advocates a "religionless Christianity." See *Honest to God*, p. 86, n. 2.

[4]"Why I Wrote It," *The Honest to God Debate*, ed. by D. L. Edwards (Philadelphia: Westminster Press, 1963), p. 279. From now on, *The Honest to God Debate* will be referred to as *HGD*. Robinson's genuine religious and Christian intention is reasserted in his latest book: *Explorations into God* (Stanford, Cal.: Stanford University Press, 1967), p. 3., but the ambiguity of his system remains unchanged.

11

less, a series of his statements undoubtedly laid the groundwork for a death-of-God theology. It is in this sense that we may consider *Honest to God* as a forerunner of the death-of-God trend.

There were, of course, many other forerunners,[5] but none of them received such wide publicity in the United States. Consequently, none of them prepared the intellectual climate for seminarians, university students, and even average "intellectual" Christians very thoroughly for the next step, the proclamation of the new gospel that "God is dead."[6]

It is also true that several death-of-God books were published before, or contemporaneously with, *Honest to God.*[7] Yet, one can still speak about the latter as a preparation for, or forerunner of the movement, since it was only after the Honest-to-God debate had made its influence felt on the American scene that the average Christian was awakened, in the second half of 1965 and the beginning of 1966, to the existence of a death-of-God theology.[8]

In the following summary of Dr. Robinson's thought I will rely primarily on *Honest to God*, but occasionally, in order to clarify or complement the meaning of his statements, I will refer to some of his later works, in particular to the concluding article "The Debate Continues," in *The Honest to God Debate* and to *The New Reformation?*[9]

---

[5] See, for instance, some bibliography in *Honest to God,* especially on pp. 26, 40.

[6] Cf., among others: "Honest to God: A Theological Appraisal," in *Religion in Life,* Winter, 1963/1964, pp. 6-51; the frequent references to it in *Christian Century,* beginning with the editorial of M. Marty, "Honest to the Church" (May 8, 1963), pp. 603-604.

[7] E.g., W. Hamilton, *The New Essence of Christianity* (New York: Association Press, 1961); Paul M. van Buren, *The Secular Meaning of the Gospel* (New York: Macmillan, 1963).

[8] The Subject Index of *Christian Century* clearly reflects the switch of interest. In 1963/1964, there are only references to *Honest to God,* whereas from July 7, 1965, on, one finds a long list of references to the "death-of-God" theology, but no articles or reviews on *Honest to God.* Cf. also the series *New Theology,* edited by Martin E. Marty and Dean G. Peerman (New York: Macmillan). No. 1, published in 1964, wrestled with issues connected with *Honest to God.* No. 2, published in 1965, concentrated on problems raised by van Buren's *The Secular Interpretation of the Gospel.*

[9] *The New Reformation?* (Philadelphia: Westminster Press, 1965).

Honest to God is not a rigorously developed theological tract, but the result of a lifelong personal struggle that has engaged both the mind and the heart of the author. He has become more and more convinced that the gulf between traditional orthodoxy and "the categories which the 'lay' world finds meaningful today," is constantly growing. In order to avoid the reduction of Christian faith to a tiny religious remnant, a thorough-going reformation is inevitable.

> . . . I believe we are being called, over the years ahead, to far more than a restating of traditional orthodoxy in modern terms. . . . A much more radical recasting, I would judge, is demanded, in the process of which the most fundamental categories of our theology—of God, of the supernatural, and of religion itself— must go into the melting (p. 7).

According to Robinson, for centuries no one has seriously doubted the three-decker structure of the universe as it has been presupposed in the Bible. God is "up there" in heaven, the earth beneath, and the waters under the earth. Even such an educated man as Luke, or such mature theologians as John and Paul, wrote most uninhibitedly of Christ "going up" or "coming down," and not even the most cultured Greeks or Romans were embarrassed by this way of thinking. For us, too, it creates little embarrassment, because we have long since made a remarkable transposition: "in place of a God who is literally or physically 'up there,' we have accepted as part of our mental furniture, a God who is spiritually or metaphysically 'out there' " (p. 12).

Today, however, although many believers do not have any problem accepting such a "projection," the image of God "out there" makes faith increasingly difficult for those who have been formed by modern scientific thinking. In order to remove this unnecessary "stumbling block," Dr. Robinson proposes, with Tillich, a new way of speaking about God. Instead of saying that God is "up or out there," we should change to a symbolism of depth: God is "the infinite and inexhaustible depth and ground of all being."[10]

In the most important chapter of his book, the Bishop makes it quite clear that by substituting "depth" for "height," he not only advocates a change in symbols, but—though tentatively and with much trepidation and hesitation—he recommends the rejection of God conceived as "another Being" or as "the highest Being above and beyond the world."[11] This world view that presents God as "a Being whose separate existence over and above the sum of things has to be demonstrated"[12] is understood by Robinson as the "supra-naturalistic cast of thought" of traditional Christianity which, he believes, no longer can be defended. He agrees with Tillich that the protest of atheism against such a God is basically correct (p. 41). The protest, according to Robinson, is twofold. Linguistic analysts claim that "God-talk" in the sense of theism is completely meaningless. The other form of protest is more aggressive; Feuerbach, Nietzsche, and J. Huxley are rather "anti-theists than atheists." For them, such a supreme Person is not only superfluous, but He is the "great enemy of man's coming of age. . . . This was the God they must 'kill' if man was not to continue dispossessed and kept in strings." Rejecting the idea of God as a supernatural Being, they felt an enormous sense of spiritual relief.[13]

Robinson, however, is not concerned with fighting supernaturalist theism. He does not want to disturb those for whom such a way of speaking about God is still satisfying. He merely intends to propose an alternative understanding of God. For him to say that God is personal is to say that

---

[10]*Honest to God,* p. 22. He quotes this from Paul Tillich, *The Shaking of the Foundations* (New York: Scribner's Sons, 1948), p. 57.

[11]This view is also retained in *The New Reformation?* pp. 114-122.

[12]Cf. also "The Debate Continues" in *HGD,* p. 256. He did not basically change his previous position.

[13]Robinson admits that the "anti-theists" have somewhat distorted the Christian idea of God, but he agrees with them that any idea of God "up there" or "out there" can and should be torn down as a useless and (for some) even harmful projection.

... personality is of *ultimate* significance in the constitution of the universe, that in personal relationships we touch the final meaning of existence as nowhere else. . . . To believe in God as love means to believe that in pure personal relationships we encounter, not merely what ought to be, but what is, the deepest, veriest truth about the structure of reality. This, in face of all the evidence, is a tremendous act of faith. But it is not the feat of persuading oneself of the existence of a super-Being beyond this world endowed with personal qualities. Belief in God is the trust, the well-nigh incredible trust, that to give ourselves to the uttermost in love is not to be confounded but to be 'accepted,' that Love is the ground of our being, to which ultimately we 'come home."[14]

Thus Robinson maintains that theology has to be translated into anthropology, that theological affirmations are not to be interpreted as a description of "the highest Being," but as affirmations about human life. A statement is theological because it affirms the ultimacy of personal relationships: "It is saying that *God,* the final truth and reality of 'deep down things,' *is* love."

He clearly perceives that his position is very close to that of Feuerbach and admits that Feuerbach's system, taken to its logical conclusion, is altogether atheistic because "it runs out into the deification of man" (p. 50). Robinson is definitely against taking this final step. Therefore, he is compelled to modify his former identification of theological statements with statements about human existence. This ought not to be understood in the sense of a simple reductionism, as if theology were nothing more than anthropology, the knowledge of God being nothing but knowledge of man. Theology concerns the *ultimate ground and depth* of human existence. It uncovers "the transcendent unconditional element in all our relationships, and supremely in our relationships with other persons" (pp. 51-52).

To assert with Saint John that "God is love" is not the same as to say that love (i.e., human love in its idealized projection)

---

[14]Cf. also *The New Reformation?* pp. 117-118.

is God. Nevertheless, "the eternal *Thou* can be met only in, with and under the finite *Thou*, whether in the encounter with other persons or in the response to the natural order."[15]

Bishop Robinson also attempts to reinterpret Christology, following the principle of Bultmannian demythologization, although, as he himself recognizes, he is more conservative in this regard than Bultmann. In Christology, too, he rejects "the supra-naturalist scheme": God the Son coming to earth from outside. As long as we think of God and man "as two beings each with distinct natures, one from the 'other side,' and one from 'this side,' then it is impossible to create from them more than a God-man, a divine visitant," who is disguised as a beggar, but is, in fact, a prince (p. 67). This primitive mythological-metaphysical presentation, in order to become credible today, needs a thorough reinterpretation.[16] Robinson proposes one by using elements of both Tillich's and Bonhoeffer's Christology.

Christ is not simply God, but a true and real man who becomes utterly transparent to God ("a window into God at work"), because He is completely freed from Himself through ultimate self-surrender in love for others on the cross. Thus Jesus is the bearer of God's final revelation only on the cross, where He becomes "so completely united to the Ground of his being that he can say, 'I and the Father are one'" (p. 74). "It is in Jesus and in Jesus alone that there is nothing of self to be seen," but only God who is love. This is how Robinson understands the traditional formula: Christ is perfect God and perfect man (pp. 76-77).

If in Jesus the Ground of our being, which is love, has been fully exposed because He has been totally and without reserve "the man for others,"[17] this same pattern must apply also to us

---

[15] At this point, Robinson quotes M. Buber, *I and Thou* (New York: Scribner's, 1958) and *Between Man and Man*.

[16] Cf. *Honest to God,* pp. 63, 67, 70. The metaphysical and the mythological, for Robinson, are only two forms of the same type of thought. Their difference, to him, seems quite negligible.

[17] This is the famous formula of D. Bonhoeffer, *The Letters and Papers from Prison* (New York: Macmillan, 1966), pp. 237-238.

sinners to whom his life, "the New Creation" in New Testament terminology, is offered as a gift. We sinners were estranged from the Ground of our being and will not be reconciled to it (Him?), unless we become a "new man in Christ Jesus," "a man for others" (pp. 77-83).

In this way, the foundations are laid for a "religionless Christianity" in the direction, as Robinson believes, of Bonhoeffer's thought. Our salvation depends on nothing specifically religious.

> Encounter with the Son of Man is spelled out in terms of an entirely 'secular' concern for food, water supplies, housing, hospitals and prisons, just as Jeremiah earlier defined the knowledge of God in terms of justice for the poor and needy.

Religion, in fact, could be the greatest barrier to a right relationship with God, since it might separate man from his fellows by secluding him into a pre-Christian privileged sphere of the Sacred (p. 61).

Yet the Bishop of Woolwich is far from discouraging us from praying or taking part in the liturgy of the Church; he merely intends to give it a "secular" interpretation. The function of the liturgy is not to help us escape from this world into another world, from the "secular" into the "religious," but to make us more sensitive to the very depth of the secular, of the common. Its purpose is "to focus, sharpen and deepen our response to the world and to other people beyond the point of proximate concern (of liking, self-interest, limited commitment, etc.) to that of ultimate concern; to purify and correct our loves in the light of Christ's love."

The Eucharistic celebration sets forth this truth "in symbol and in power." The bread and wine we use in the service "are samples only of all other common things and the focus of all other common relationships. . . . The Holy Communion is the point at which the common . . . becomes the carrier of the unconditional." It proclaims that "the presence of Christ with his people is tied to a right receiving of the common, to a right relationship with one's neighbor" (pp. 85-99).

Prayer, too, receives a "non-religious" interpretation. To pray for another is to open oneself to another unconditionally in love. If we take the otherness of the other person most seriously, if we accept him "without reservation," we let God into that relationship: we are with him in the presence of God. "It may not be talking to God as though to a third person about him at all"; it may not be a specifically religious or consciously Christian act, yet "it may be a meeting of Christ in that man" (pp. 99-100).

At this point, I do not intend to give a critical evaluation of *Honest to God*. Many have already performed this work with competence and objectivity.[18] It can, for instance, be shown that the Bible does not speak about God as literally "up there." The same Saint Paul who uses the symbols of height so "uninhibitedly," also adapts the stoic image of God filling the universe to Christian usage and speaks about the Spirit and Christ dwelling in us.[19] The riches of patristic tradition also seem to be completely unknown to Robinson. Saint Augustine's God, to take just one example, is at once "the highest and closest, most hidden and most present"; He is closer to man than his own deepest self and higher than the highest of man.[20] We could also point out the gross confusion between mythological and metaphysical ways of thinking; Robinson implies that the personal God of metaphysics is nothing more than "a sophisticated version of the old man in the sky."[21]

---

[18]Cf., first of all, E. L. Mascall, *The Secularization of Christianity* (New York: Holt, 1966), and E. Schillebeeckx, *Personale Begegnung mit Gott. Eine Antwort an John A. T. Robinson* (Mainz: Matthias-Gruenwald, 1964); *Neues Glaubenverständnis. Honest to Robinson* (Mainz: Matthias-Gruenwald, 1964). See also the articles quoted under nn. 19, 21. A German collection of reviews concerning the book: *Diskussion zu Bischof Robinsons Gott ist anders,* Hrsg. von Hermann Walter Augustin (München: Kaiser, 1964).

[19]Cf. Daniel Jenkins, "Religion and Coming of Age," in *HGD*, pp. 208-209.

[20]Cf. *Confessions*, VI, 4, and III, 11.

[21]Cf. David Jenkins, "Concerning Theism," in *HGD*, p. 195, and a review by H. McCabe in *HGD*, pp. 165-180.

However, my only concern here is to determine the place of *Honest to God* in the death-of-God controversy. On the one hand, it prepares the intellectually alert, average Christian for the death-of-God debate; on the other hand, to judge by the enthusiastic response of those to whom "it has (seemingly, at least) given back God," the book has touched upon the nerve of contemporary religious sensitivity.[22] *Honest to God* truly stands at a crossroads. From Robinson's position, it is extremely easy, both logically and psychologically, to develop a death-of-God theology by drawing the legitimate conclusions from some of his basic assertions; whereas, if the genuinely religious insights of the book (which are not rarely quite inconsistent with the former series of affirmations) were further clarified and expanded, they could serve as a valuable contribution to a relevant contemporary theology of God. The following pages will attempt to substantiate this statement.

The crucial point in Robinson's system is what he means by the Tillichian "depth" or "ground of being." As has been seen above, he affirms again and again that God is not a Being above or beyond the universe. Such a God is a supra-naturalist "projection" which we have to be prepared to discard. On the other hand, Robinson tries hard to exclude naturalism and pantheism. In fact, he never explicitly identifies God with nature, but avoids spelling out their relationship by referring to God as the depth of nature. Thus the symbol, unexplained, remains ambiguous. Not even in his two new books, *The New Reformation?* and *Explorations into God*, does he achieve any substantial clarification.[23]

This ambiguity is confirmed by examining his analysis of the depth of personal relationships and of prayer. It is not at all clear what he understands by the "unconditional," which we

---

[22]See "Some Readers' Letters" in *HGD*, pp. 51-81.

[23]It must be admitted, however, that he emphasizes more than in *Honest to God* "the centrality of the utterly *personal* relationship of communion with God summed up in Jesus' address, 'Abba, Father' " (*The New Reformation?* p. 13).

can meet only "in, with and under" the condition of human relationship. Sometimes he seems to affirm with Feuerbach that true religion "consists in acknowledging the divinity of the attributes" of man, such as love, wisdom, and justice, "not in transferring them to an illegitimate subject" who is distinct from the world (p. 50).[24] The only purpose of worship is to deepen and purify our love for our fellowmen; and the essential point in prayer is to take seriously the otherness of a human person whom I encounter.

Thus, it becomes understandable why the death-of-God theologians and Robinson feel close to each other, in spite of their openly stated divergencies. Having read *The Secular Meaning of the Gospel* by van Buren, the Bishop seems delighted that his prophecy came true: ". . . in retrospect *Honest to God* will be seen to have erred in not being nearly radical enough."[25] Van Buren also notices that he finds much similarity between his own secular interpretation of the Gospel and that of Bishop Robinson.[26] Nor is it incidental that Altizer, when asked at a public debate how he would envision the function of prayer in his system which proclaims the death of the transcendent God, referred to the chapter on "A 'Non-Religious' Understanding of Prayer" in *Honest to God* as being closest to his own ideas on the matter.[27] In fact, only one more step is required to eliminate all talk about divine transcendence[28] and affirm, as Altizer does, that the new higher

---

[24]See L. Feuerbach, *The Essence of Christianity*, p. 21.

[25]"The Debate Continues" in *HGD*, p. 250. While excited by the "brilliantly original thesis," the Bishop is also disturbed by van Buren's book and issues his "caveats." See "The Debate Continues" in *HGD*, pp. 250-253; *The New Reformation?* p. 24.

[26]*Cf.* van Buren, *op. cit.*, p. 200, n. 5. Also see the bibliography in T. J. J. Altizer and W. Hamilton, *Radical Theology and the Death of God* (Indianapolis: Bobbs Merrill, 1966), p. 200. It classifies *Honest to God* as "radical theology in Europe."

[27]This statement was made by Altizer during *A Workshop on the Problem of God in Contemporary Thought* (The Catholic University of America, June 12-23, 1967) in Seminar I.

[28]Robinson still tries to maintain divine transcendence by explaining our relationship to the Ground of our being as a relationship in freedom, a freedom which implies total dependence. See *Honest to God*, pp. 130-131.

form of the Sacred is without remainder and exclusively immanent in this world, dialectically identical with it.

Then, of course, Christ will be only "the man for others" without being "a window into God," a perfect expression of an unambiguously and exclusively human love.

There is also a close kinship as to the understanding of the essence of Christian life: imitating Jesus who sets us free from self to serve others, according to P. van Buren; serving Jesus who is disguised in our brothers, according to W. Hamilton; and promoting the realization of the "Great Humanity Divine," which is the "totally incarnate Word," in the view of T. Altizer. Both Robinson and the death-of-God theologians agree on one basic point: there is no room in their system for a life oriented toward, and fulfilled by, communion with a transcendent God, no room for a life dedicated to the service, praise, and worship of God for His own sake.

What we have discussed so far is, however, only one aspect of Bishop Robinson's theology. We cannot deny the evidence of the many letters which prove that his book has evoked a powerful religious response from those who, tormented by doubts about their conventional patterns of thinking about God, experienced a profound sense of relief upon reading *Honest to God*. It is undoubtedly true that the book does not do justice to the biblical doctrine of God, nor to the richness of patristic and (authentic) scholastic tradition. What Robinson presents is a caricature of traditional Christian theism, but this caricature seems to be his honest understanding of it, and—as shown by the reaction of many of his readers—the honest understanding of a large segment of contemporary Christians. God conceived of as *a* Being among others, being above everything, yet apparently of the same order as the rest; God as not only distinct but *separate* from the world, spatially or quasi-spatially located "out there" constitutes, indeed, a very real obstacle to faith. The fact that many have been convinced that they ought to think of God in this way shows the urgent need for purifying and deepening our current popular theism, although, of course, in a less ambiguous and philosophically more accurate way than the Bishop of Woolwich has done. In altogether rejecting without qualification the "supra-naturalistic cast of thought," he has presented the premises for a pantheistic conclusion.

Another aspect of Robinson's thought ought to be positively evaluated: his analysis of personal relationships can be further clarified and developed as a way of knowing God that would probably strongly appeal to contemporary man.[29] The man of the age of technology has some difficulty with appreciating the cosmological argument for the existence of God, however true it may be objectively. His overwhelming experience of dominating and "creating" the outside world as his own possession obscures his awareness of the world's origin in, and its fundamental dependence upon God. But being continually threatened in his personal existence by the very world he has created, he is extremely sensitive to the value and implications of personal encounter. This is perhaps one of the reasons Robinson's book had such an immediate religious impact on many of his readers. His insufficient and reductionist explanations aside, he sometimes finds a powerful, genuinely religious language to describe the sacred dimension of personal love relationships:

> Our convictions about love and its ultimacy are not projections from human love; rather our sense of the sacredness of love derives from the fact that in this relationship as nowhere else there is disclosed and laid bare the divine Ground of all our being (p. 53) . . . .

---

[29]Before *Honest to God,* there had been many thinkers like M. Buber (e.g., *I and Thou,* New York: Scribner's, 1958) and Hans Urs von Balthasar (e.g., *Science, Religion and Christianity,* London: Burns and Oates, 1958) who analyzed, more in depth than Robinson, the religious implications of personal relationships. But none of them succeeded in stirring up interest in such a wide audience as *Honest to God.* The analysis, however, is far from finished.

The way through to the vision of the Son of man and the knowledge of God which is the heart of contemplative prayer, is by unconditional love of the neighbor, of 'the nearest *Thou* at hand' (p. 100).

Thus the position of the Bishop of Woolwich is truly ambivalent. He stands at a theological crossroads from whence two opposite directions may be taken.[30] He has prepared the stage for the death-of-God theology on the one hand, and on the other he has also given hints and insights (however ambiguously they may have been formulated) which can contribute to a renewed theology of God.

---

[30]The appraisal of A. MacIntyre, an atheist himself, does not take into account the inconsistency of Robinson's thought and his fundamental intention: "What is striking about Dr. Robinson's book"—he writes—"is first and foremost that he is an atheist" ("God and the Theologians" in *HDG*, p. 215).

RADICAL THEOLOGY

2

WILLIAM HAMILTON

William Hamilton is the least original among the representatives of radical theology. He lacks the mystical fervor and apologetic vision of Altizer, the passionless cold logic of van Buren's systematic mind. Yet, since his ideas seem to be the most easily assimilable by the average reader, his interpretation of the "death-of-God" slogan comes closest to what some American Christians experience today. Almost everyone who corresponded with Altizer, even when empathizing with his basic intuition, pressed him for further clarification on many specific points which the writer could not understand. But most of those who favor Hamilton's position congratulate him because he expressed what they deeply felt but were either unable or too timid to put into words. For instance, a Presbyterian minister wrote him enthusiastically: "You put into words what I discover I believe and you do it so clearly that I can say to others, this is what I believe but have not been able to formulate adequately."[1] A former minister, now an English teacher, became again vitally interested in religion through reading an article by Hamilton: "I'm wholly in sympathy with your declaration that God is dead. If I were to express my own deepest feelings on the subject, I couldn't do better than borrow your own straightforward expression."[2]

---

[1] *The Death of God Debate,* ed. by Jackson Lee Ice and John J. Carey (Philadelphia: The Westminster Press, 1967), p. 164.
[2] *Ibid.,* pp. 174-175.

In the first part of his career, Hamilton lived, taught, and wrote more or less comfortably in "that good old world of middle-of-the-road, ecumenical neo-orthodoxy."[3] At that time, his idea of God appears to have been a curious amalgam of the popular understanding of the Barthian wholly other "enemy-God," of the "problem-solving" and "need-fulfilling" God of the American religious pragmatism, and of Jesus, the suffering God as presented in the writings of Reinhold Niebuhr.[4] The prevailing image in his mind was, however, that of the terror-striking Barthian God. This God of "the biblical-Augustinian Reformed" tradition, Hamilton affirms, cannot be known by man, but He makes himself known in Scripture and meets man in critical historical events. We can hardly "speak about Him," but we can speak "to Him"; we can praise, worship, and adore Him.[5] *The New Essence of Christianity* in which these statements appear is the first, and so far only, major work of Hamilton. It was first published in 1961 and contains those "fragments" of Christianity which the neoorthodox Hamilton could at that time personally accept.[6]

However, already at this stage the author's uneasiness about his "correct doctrine of God"[7] is evident. In the face of suffering, which Hamilton analyzes in *The Plague* by A. Camus, the biblical God appears cold and indifferent. He begins to suspect that this wholly other God "is not only remote, he is irrelevant. He not only is far from us, he has departed from us. It is a very short step, but a critical one, to move from the

---

[3]He was born in 1924 at Evanston, Illinois. A Baptist, he studied at the Union Theological Seminary, at Princeton University, and at the University of St. Andrew. He received degrees in the arts and theology and a doctorate in philosophy. He has been professor of systematic and historical theology at Colgate Rochester Theological School, New York, since 1955. He recently joined the faculty of New College in Sarasota, Florida.

[4]See "The Shape of a Radical Theology," *Frontier Theology,* ed. by Dean Peerman (Richmond, Va.: J. Knox, 1967), pp. 69-71.

[5]*The New Essence of Christianity* was published first in 1961; the revised edition appeared in 1966 (New York: Associate Press) with a preface by J. A. T. Robinson. See pp. 35-42.

[6]*Ibid.,* p. 13.

[7]*Ibid.,* p. 36.

otherness of God to the absence of God. But this is what the problem of suffering tempts some to do. Many are saying, not out of confidence or pride, but out of a kind of exhausted sadness, much like that of Dr. Rieux, 'perhaps this other God is not'."[8]

At this point, nevertheless, Hamilton is still fighting for belief in God. He still holds that a Christian "cannot live as a Christian for long with the suspicion that God himself has withdrawn."[9] He admits that, for many, our time is a time of the death of God, yet he believes not only that God "will come, in his own time, to the broken and contrite heart, if we continue to offer that to him," but he is also convinced, in 1961, of the following:

> Neither "death of God," "absence of God," nor disappearance of God is wholly adequate to describe the full meaning of our religious situation. . . . In one sense God seems to have withdrawn from the world and its sufferings, and this leads us to accuse him of either irrelevance or cruelty. But in another sense, he is experienced as a pressure and a wounding from which we would love to be free. For many of us who call ourselves Christians, therefore, believing in the time of the "death of God" means that he is there when we do not want him, in ways we do not want him, and he is not there when we do want him.[10]

But this absent-present disturber God, the One who is experienced as an afflicting withdrawal and as a wounding presence, becomes bearable for Hamilton—because of Jesus. Jesus as the suffering Lord radically corrects and transforms the idea of the terrifying divinity which Hamilton cannot bear:

> In Jesus the Lord we see for the first time what Christian "divinity" must be taken to be: it is God withdrawing from all claims to power and authority and sovereignty, and consenting to become himself the victim and subject of all that the world can

---

[8]*Ibid.*, p. 55.
[9]*Ibid.*, p. 59.
[10]*Ibid.*, pp. 64-65.

do. The afflicting God of our previous chapter [in *The New Essence of Christianity*] becomes now the afflicted God. Divinity in Jesus is not withdrawal from the world; it is full consent to abide in the world, and to allow the world to have its way with it.[11]

Hamilton concedes that the two concepts—"the afflicting God" and "the afflicted God"—cannot be reconciled. He does not even attempt this.[12] For the time being, the suffering Jesus safeguards his wavering belief in God.

One can discern a turning point in Hamilton's position in 1964/65. One of the major influences in shaping his new stand was the "religionless interpretation of Christianity" by Bonhoeffer, whom Hamilton had studied since 1952. Probably in connection with his studies on Bonhoeffer, Hamilton discovered a new relationship of man to the world. Man can no longer feel the awesome presence of God in a world which has become the building material for man's own creation.[13]

Another blow to his shattered faith in God came in a television panel. He had to play the Christian in competition with "two able professionals, a personnel man and a psychiatrist." He was supposed to show how God and Christianity work as a problem-solver concerning a tragic incident which resulted from an argument between husband and wife: "I forget what I actually said; something rhetorical and dishonest, no doubt. It was a rotten television program. I was shaken, and Christianity as problem-solving and need-fulfilling died for me on that day."[14]

"The last of the trivial events" which moved him into his present radical position was "the experience of turning 40."[15]

---

[11]*Ibid.*, pp. 90-92.

[12]*Ibid.*, p. 95.

[13]See W. Hamilton, "A Note on Radical Theology," *Concilium* (New York: Paulist Press, 1967), XXIX, 93-95; *The Death of God Debate*, pp. 217-218; "The Shape of a Radical Theology," p. 70.

[14]W. Hamilton, "The Shape of a Radical Theology," p. 70.

[15]*Ibid.*, p. 71.

In an interview with a reporter from *The New Yorker,* he declares: "I am beginning to feel that the time has come for me to put up or shut up, for me to be an in or an out."[16] He needed "to make things happen" rather than just letting things happen to him. Thus under the pressure of the incoming middle age, with a last flare-up of his youthful energies, he began to proclaim the death of God and hoped to start "some movement."[17]

It is nevertheless hard to describe what he means by this slogan. When he speaks as a spokesman for the "movement," as a close comrade-in-arms of Altizer who is the only other representative of the movement, he stresses that the " 'death of God' is not merely private, subjective, psychological. It points to something that has taken place in the world of reality."[18] "It is a public event in our history."[19] It started with "the coming of Jesus, as the self-emptying of God." The Incarnation is "the enabling part" of this event. But:

> The nineteenth century is that time when the death itself is predicted, believed in, lived out. The Christian God, in Europe and America, is dying by departing wholly from the world (deism) or collapsing into the world (romanticism, Marx, Ibsen) between 1789 and 1941. . . . But there is a third part of the "when" answer, and that is now, here, mid-twentieth-century America. . . . There is something about our time and place that is making the event prepared by the incarnation and analyzed by the nineteenth century come home. The twentieth century is proving to be a time when the "death of God" can be affirmed without guilt, fear, or sadness.[20]

When he seems to speak more for himself, he is eager to ad-

---

[16]Quoted in Ved Mehta, *The New Theologian* (New York: Harper & Row, 1965), p. 142.

[17]"The Shape of a Radical Theology," pp. 71-72.

[18]*The Death of God Debate,* p. 219.

[19]W. Hamilton, "The Death of God Theologies Today," *Radical Theology and the Death of God* (New York: Bobbs-Merrill, 1966), p. 47.

[20]*The Death of God Debate,* pp. 215-216.

mit that "as 'event,' in a literal historical sense, 'death of God' is neither serviceable nor intelligible." It is rather a metaphor which points to the experience of a particular group of modern Western (especially American) Christians today.[21] The metaphor means more than the dialectic of the absence and presence of God to which he had still clung in *The New Essence of Christianity*. It means that God no longer makes himself known: "we do not know, do not adore, do not possess, do not believe in God."[22] "A real loss, something irretrievable is portrayed by the metaphor of death."[23] The God whom we have lost is both the transcendent "enemy-God" of neoorthodoxy and God the need-fulfiller. Although even in this new stage Jesus occupies the center of Hamilton's thought, he is no longer conceived of as the suffering Lord or the "afflicted God"; he is merely and simply man, "the man for others" of Bonhoeffer without the mystique of transcendence this title implied for Bonhoeffer.

If one compares all the different statements about the meaning of the "death of God," the position of Hamilton appears rather inconsistent and ambiguous. On the one hand, he states with a cold objectivity "the breakdown of the religious *a priori*":

> . . . there is no way, ontological, cultural or psychological, to locate a part of the self or a part of human experience that needs God. There is no God-shaped blank within man. . . . It is not true to say that there are certain areas, problems, dimensions to life today that can only be faced, solved, illumined, dealt with, by a religious perspective.[24]

---

[21]See "A Note on Radical Theology," p. 92; "The Shape of a Radical Theology," p. 73.

[22]"The Death of God Theologies Today," p. 28.

[23]"The Shape of a Radical Theology," p. 73.

[24]"The Death of God Theologies Today," p. 40. G. Vahanian, in his unjustly forgotten book *The Death of God: The Culture of Our Post-Christian Era* (New York: Braziller, 1961), describes brilliantly that popular religious attitude which explains the notion of the "need-fulfiller God" in Hamilton's thought. When applying this attitude in general to the average American, his statements, in my opinion, cannot be validated,

On the other hand, his most widely known definition of what he means by the "death of God" flatly contradicts his statement I quoted above: "We are not talking about the absence of the experience of God, but about the experience of the absence of God."[25] If we experience the absence of God and experience it as a "real loss," this seems to indicate that there is nevertheless "some part of the self"—to use the vague formulation of Hamilton—which truly needs God. How could we feel the absence of someone who is completely irrelevant to us?

Moreover, whether we consider the "death of God" as a "public event" affecting the nature of the world, or as a group-experience, it still remains unclear what all this implies for God himself. There was a time when "having a god was appropriate, possible, even necessary. But now is not such a time."[26] This distinguishes the stand of the radical theologian from that of an atheist. But does this mean that God has now withdrawn, or that he is on vacation and will perhaps return, or that he truly died as a man dies? Perhaps Hamilton shares, but never states, the philosophical presupposition of Altizer: God exists

---

but they seem to be correct about a certain specific religious trend in American culture. There are believers who really have only "faith in Faith," but no faith in the Christian God. This "faith," nevertheless, is necessary for them, because "it works." It assures them peace, success, psychic balance. Whom he believes in is, in fact, a secondary question. In any case, it must be a God who reliably serves man: a "porter" who carries his burdens, a "cosmic pal" who can only love, but cannot punish (pp. 195, 74). In the measure, however, that civilization develops, the immanent God-idol of modern man inevitably loses ground. The institutions of modern society, the more and more sophisticated industrial production fulfills the needs of the petty bourgeois more reliably than the "God" advertised at Sunday services. The "God-hypothesis" becomes more and more superfluous as science discovers the missing links in the empirical causal series that explain the phenomena of nature (see G. Vahanian, "Theology and 'The End of the Age of Religion,'" *Concilium* (New York: Paulist Press, 1961), XVI, 99-110. If we now apply this line of thought to the radical theology of Hamilton, it can be interpreted as a radical protest against a pious hypocrisy; it states frankly and openly, albeit in a confused language, what some pastors never dared to confess to themselves: "God," the manipulable servant of man's needs, is dead.

[25]*Ibid.*, p. 28.
[26]*The Death of God Debate*, p. 214.

"objectively" as long as, and in the form in which, man is conscious of him. Altizer explicitly identifies the objective and the subjective sphere: his God is a God of human consciousness, depending for his existence on human consciousness. Hamilton never states whether he agrees on this point with his friend. Perhaps he has never formulated the question either.

Not much clearer is Hamilton's attitude concerning the future of God. He insists that the loss of God is irretrievable; the radical theologians are "men who do not anticipate his return." They are "without faith as well as without hope."[27] But in the same article, "Thursday's Child," some lines below, he declares that he hopes and waits "in a kind of prayer for the losses to be returned." He does not expect, however, the return of the threatening "enemy-God of Barth, nor the need-fulfiller God of the average Christian, but a God in whom we will find delight and joy."[28] Yet, as his radical position is more and more elaborated, his hope in God's return fades away. But surprisingly, even in one of his latest, most unequivocal statements, after he repudiated his previous position which admitted of some hope of God's return, he still maintains the possibility that in the future, radical theology "could move to the right and the birth or resurrection of God could be experienced."[29]

But even if God himself will not be resurrected, Hamilton is convinced that some experience of the sacred, a "godless sacred," will undoubtedly survive. He cannot as yet predict what concrete shape the sacred, which does not need a theistic explanation, will take. He suggests, nonetheless, that perhaps "an experience of sex" can become a kind of sacred event for some today.[30]

[27]See W. Hamilton, "The Shape of a Radical Theology Today," p. 73; "American Theology, Radicalism and the Death of God"; "Thursday's Child," *Radical Theology and the Death of God*, pp. 7, 92.

[28]"The Death of God Theologies Today," p. 41.

[29]*The Death of God Debate*, pp. 238-239.

[30]See *Ibid.*, pp. 226-227. He gives as an example of "sacred event" a sexual relationship outside marriage as described in *The Scarlet Letter*, and interpreted by Hugh Hefner.

In spite of his fluctuating mood between the sense of an ir-revocable loss of God and a prayerful hope for his return, one point has always remained firm in Hamilton's creed. In the time of the "death of God," the Christian must go out from the cloister to the world, from the Church to the City. In this move-ment, Hamilton believes, radical theology revitalizes a genuine aspect of the Protestant tradition. As last century's liberal Prot-estantism vindicated the rights of the autonomous religious personality against the tyranny of the institution, as neo-orthodox Protestantism reaffirmed the principle of justification through faith in a righteous God—both implicit in Luther's life and doctrine—so today we are discovering the central ethical implication of Luther's move from the cloister, from the "place of protection and security, of crder and beauty, to the bustling middle-class world of the new university, of politics, princes and peasants. The place of the radical Protestant today is be-side the neighbor, beside the enemy, at the disposal of the man in need."[31] This stand with the neighbor in the world is not just "sheer atheist humanism," since its motive is "obedience to Jesus himself."[32] The radical Christian is defined, therefore, as the man "bound to Jesus, obedient to him and obedient as he was obedient."[33]

Hamilton, of course, is aware of the objection of his critics: why has he chosen Jesus as the object of his obedience? Is there some special reason why it should be Jesus, and not Albert Camus or Martin Luther King or Francis of Assisi? If Jesus is not the Son of God, how can he be the center and the ultimate norm of one's life? Is a christology justified without theology, i.e., without a doctrine on God? Is Hamilton's choice not a completely arbitrary one? He can only reply that his com-mitment to Jesus has been "freely made." (This, in fact, has not been questioned by anyone. A free choice still can be an

---

[31]"The Death of God Theologies Today," pp. 36-37.
[32]*Ibid.*, p. 48.
[33]"The Shape of a Radical Theology," p. 74.

arbitrary choice.) He affirms that "there is something there, in his words, his life, his way with others, his death, that I do not find elsewhere. I am drawn, and I have given my allegiance."[34]

Hamilton's obedience to Jesus entails a double task: Jesus may be concealed in the world, in the neighbor, in this struggle for justice, in that struggle for beauty, clarity, order. The life of the world is like a Halloween party, and the Christian has to strip off the masks of the world to find Jesus, and "finding him to stay with him and do his work."[35]

The other task of the Christian in the world is more dangerous and, therefore, even more challenging. Beyond unmasking Jesus in the neighbor, some of us may be "called" [by whom?] to follow Luther's imperative: "become [yourself] a Christ to your neighbor!" In this form, Christian life "is not so active and worldly"; it is not "a looking outwards to the world and its claims," but rather "a look within in order to become Jesus."[36] The language of Hamilton seems to suggest here more than an ethical imitation of Christ; it points to a mystical identification with him. This is the only context wherein the overwhelmingly ethical position of Hamilton approaches the closest to the panchristic mysticism of Altizer.

All this movement of going out from the Church to the world is presented with a naive optimism which received impetus in 1965 by the program of the "Great Society," and by the seeming success of the civil rights movement. Hamilton believed, at least in 1965, in an apparently unlimited progress of mankind: human misery, rather than forcing one to seek refuge in God, as it did before, will challenge the post-modern man eventually to overcome it. Hamilton's faith in the success of human endeavor, a success due to the death of God, made his theology deliberately optimistic. He also hoped that the death-

---

[34]*Ibid.*, p. 75.
[35]"The Death of God Theologies Today," pp. 49-50.
[36]*Ibid.*, p. 50.

of-God theology would become a powerful movement, since it so daringly expressed the prevailing mood of our age.[37] Later, in 1967, his optimistic outlook concerning human progress and the future of his own theology had become much more guarded. He acknowledges now that there are some real evils which cannot be overcome; they can only be coped with. Even the failure or success of radical theology "is still a matter for determination. For living and thinking as a Christian without God is, to say the least, an odd and difficult aim."[38]

---

[37] W. Hamilton, "The New Optimism from Prufrock to Ringo," *Radical Theology and the Death of God,* pp. 157-170.

[38] "A Note on Radical Theology," p. 95.

3

THOMAS J. J. ALTIZER

Thomas J. J. Altizer has been the most widely advertised representative of the "death-of-God" group.[1] His apocalyptic fervor and his apparently absolute faith in his own prophetic mission have drawn immediate reactions of passionate enthusiasm or equally passionate rejection in the audiences he addressed. Altizer's theology is rather a powerful vision than an "objective rational analysis."[2] His ideal, whom he likes to present as the great forerunner of "radical Christianity," is William Blake, the poet and apocalyptic seer who creates a mythology of his own. Therefore, if we want to penetrate the works of Altizer, we have to take them for what they are: a strange blending of theological-philosophical reasoning with a certain "mystical" vision expressed in a highly poetic and mythological language. He wants to preach, first of all, a message, a "gospel." He is convinced that his vocation is to proclaim (and thereby accelerate) the coming of a new era in the history of Christianity, or, more precisely, to cooperate in bringing about a new stage in the cosmic process of divine self-development.

Although at first reading his thought seems rather compli-

---

[1]Altizer is a native of Cambridge, Massachusetts, and an Episcopalian layman. He received the degrees of A.B., A.M., and Ph.D. at the University of Chicago. Since 1961 he has been associate professor of Bible and Religion at Emory University, Atlanta, Ga.

[2]"The Waning Death of God Tumult," *Christianity Today,* May 26, 1967, pp. 16-19.

cated and hardly understandable, there are, it seems to me, two clues which can provide us with access to the fundamental thrust of his "theology." The first clue is Altizer's original experience of the sacred as absolutely opposed to the profane. This experience, as it is analyzed in his first major work, *Oriental Mysticism and Biblical Eschatology,*[3] is based on a fusion of the Kierkegaardian and early Barthian absolute dialectic between God and creature with the categories of Oriental mysticism.

The second clue to Altizer's later works is his peculiar way of understanding the Hegelian dialectic process. The discovery of Hegel revolutionizes his thought, determines its movement and provides it with a certain structure and coherence in spite of its exuberant imagery and "logical imprecisions" (which even Hamilton, his close friend and admirer, is compelled to acknowledge).[4] The influence of Hegel can already be discerned in *Mircea Eliade and the Dialectic of the Sacred.*[5] It becomes, however, more and more evident in *The Gospel of Christian Atheism*[6] and in his latest book *The New Apocalypse: The Radical Christian Vision of William Blake.*[7]

The primordial experience of an absolute and irreconcilable contradiction between the reality of the sacred and the reality of this world, or between religious consciousness and profane consciousness (two spheres which are never clearly distinguished in his mind), is of decisive importance for the early Altizer. He believes that this contradiction is particularly characteristic of our time: "We moderns are immersed in a profane world that charges the immediate moment with absolute meaning and value. To us, religion can appear only as an alien reality. In our sensibility, the religious Reality can manifest itself only as the other."[8] Yet the opposition, Altizer attempts to show, is

---

[3] Philadelphia: Westminster, 1961.
[4] William Hamilton, "The Death of God Theologies Today," p. 31.
[5] Philadelphia: Westminster, 1963.
[6] Philadelphia: Westminster, 1966.
[7] Lansing: Michigan State University Press, 1967.
[8] Thomas J. J. Altizer, *Oriental Mysticism and Biblical Eschatology,* p. 9.

not restricted to the present moment of our history, though the "wholly profane world of modern culture helps one to understand it fully"; it characterizes both biblical eschatology and the highest forms of Oriental mysticism.[9]

Israel discovered the full meaning of the deity of Yahweh only "through an 'emptying of the reality' of the world." The more she became aware of Yahweh's sacred reality, the more she was forced to reject the reality of this world.[10] The negation of the world culminates in the message of Jesus. Altizer agrees with Nietzsche that Jesus understood "everything natural, temporal, spatial, historical only as signs, as occasions for parables" of inner realities. Thus the genuine Christian proclamation "represents an instinctive hatred of every reality"; it is "the ultimate form of rebellion, the absolute form of self-negation."[11]

Later, Christianity lost "the purity of its eschatological experience"[12] and "succumbed to a this-worldly and ultimately irreligious paganism in its positive evaluation of life in the world. It partially absorbed a Dionysian attempt to transfigure and say yes to life."[13] In addition, the Kingdom of God was relegated to the sphere of the eternal spiritual that exists above the world so that it no longer threatens to destroy "the realities of profane existence."[14]

After the analysis of the "original" eschatological message of Christianity, Altizer moves on to study the various forms of Buddhist teaching and practice. His conclusion, although it seems to result from a detailed examination of the historical development of the Buddhist movement, is surprisingly simple: the attitude of the Buddhist toward the Reality of the Sacred and the reality of this world is basically the same as that of

---

[9]*Ibid.*, p. 190.
[10]*Ibid.*, p. 78.
[11]*Ibid.*, p. 107.
[12]*Ibid.*, p. 112.
[13]*Ibid.*, p. 109.
[14]*Ibid.*, p. 111.

the "genuine" Christian. Both the Buddhist and the Christian are called "into a new and immediate participation in the sacred Reality." This sacred Reality, the kingdom of God for the Christian, Nirvana for the Buddhist, demands "the extinction of everything that we know as life and self"; it is "the annihilation of all other reality whatsoever."[15]

Evidently, this has also far-reaching consequences for the field of ethics: in Altizer's view, there is no real difference between the compassion taught in Mahayana Buddhism and Christian charity. Radical love, i.e., self-giving, is possible only in a vision that considers the self and every worldly reality as ultimately unreal. "It is precisely because the self is unreal that it can be given to the other." As pure Christian charity was originally grounded in an eschatological hope of the imminent annihilation of this world, likewise the compassion of the Buddhist is directly proportionate to his perceiving the ultimate void of all distinct experiential reality, including selfhood and consciousness. Since, in the ultimate analysis, all distinction among beings and all self-asserting consciousness are an illusion and things are basically one, compassion that implies a radical giving up of self is the most authentic response to the nature of Ultimate Reality.[16]

Altizer will later modify this oversimplified identification of "genuine" Christianity with "genuine" Oriental mysticism, yet even in his last work he retains a fundamentally monistic view of reality and a conception of love which is grounded on the unreality of personal selfhood.

One can perhaps see now how Altizer's early experience of the sacred and the profane foreshadows his later death-of-God vision. The irreconcilable enmity between profane consciousness and the consciousness of sacred Reality constantly threatens to eliminate one of the two poles. Altizer still affirms

---

[15]*Ibid.*, p. 124.
[16]*Ibid.*, p. 150. Altizer criticizes H. de Lubac because de Lubac distinguished Christian charity from the "compassion" of the Buddhist. Cf. *ibid.*, p. 149.

the sacred with a "religious rebellion" against a this-worldly existence which he envisions as "essentially sinful." But the very violence of his attack upon our world indicates that, in the long run, he will not be able to endure the mutually exclusive "great Either-Or of the sacred or the profane." He is too sensitive to the values of a secular existence, too much filled with life, energy, and buoyant vitality to remain on the side of what he can see only as a total (ontological) negation of our world and life. He agrees with Nietzsche "who most clearly saw that the mode of existence of the authentically modern man demanded the death of God." He admits that he shares this experience; for him, too, religious reality can manifest itself only as Nothingness. Yet he still desperately hangs on to the reality of this Nothingness and tries to affirm the ultimate unreality of our world.[17] The tension, however, becomes unbearable: Altizer had to find some way to reconcile the opposing poles. And he found it in the dialectic of Hegel: the absolute static contradiction between sacred and profane is dissolved into a relative and dynamic one: it becomes only a temporary phase which in virtue of the dialectic process of affirmation, negation, and synthesis, will be totally overcome in the future of the self-developing Reality.

In his next book, *Mircea Eliade and the Dialectic of the Sacred*, there is already present the first sketch of his death-of-God theology.[18] Altizer is more in love with the sacred than ever before. But he realizes now that the primordial sacred has been irretrievably and definitely lost for the man of our age. The line of development is irreversible. Therefore, he no longer attacks the godless, profane, this-worldly existence of modern man. On the contrary, he fully accepts it also for himself and proclaims with prophetic fervor: "We must recognize that the death of God is a historical event: God has died in *our*

---

[17]Cf. *ibid.*, pp. 190-199.

[18]Altizer is concerned not so much with interpreting faithfully the thought of Eliade, but with using his ideas as a spring-board to develop for the first time his vision of "the death of God."

time, in *our* history, in *our* existence."[19]

He can adopt this new perspective because he no longer looks at the contradiction between sacred and profane as static and absolute, but as two subsequent stages of a dialectic process. He believes that the radical affirmation of the profane is the only way to accelerate the coming of a higher stage in which the radically profane and the radically sacred will coincide in a new synthesis.[20] It is only within the framework of this dialectic that one can understand the strange claim of Altizer: the death of God is the Gospel, "the good news for our time." The more thoroughly we accept, the more firmly we will the death of God, the sooner a new epiphany of the sacred, the final coincidence and fusion of God and the world, will dawn upon us. Therefore, the radical theologian welcomes with joy the profane darkness of today's existence, since he hastens thereby the end of the night.[21] Evidently, every kind of traditional theology, all the traditional moral values associated with the Christian God, have collapsed. Theology today must "negate itself," must dwell in the night, outside of the Church, without celebrating the sacraments, without the comfort of prayer and the joy of the Holy Spirit until the dawn comes.[22]

The formal law of dialectic determines also the meaning of the Incarnation in his "system." The death of God was effected, he affirms, by the Incarnation and Crucifixion. The transcendent almighty Lord, the wholly other, the totally alien, the source of all guilt and repression, passes over into his own opposite in Christ. God truly becomes flesh; transcendence changes into immanence; God, into man Thus, for him, the Incarnation is a "movement in God himself," so that "the God who has given himself eternally for man, has thereby ceased to exist as a self-enclosed and autonomous Being."[23] The Cruci-

---

[19]"America and the Future of Theology," *Radical Theology and the Death of God*, p. 11.
[20]*Ibid.*, p. 19.
[21]See Thomas J. J. Altizer, *The Gospel of Christian Atheism*, pp. 15-18.
[22]See "America and the Future of Theology," pp. 14-15.
[23]*The Gospel of Christian Atheism*, p. 72.

fixion is the culmination of the Incarnation, since "only in the Crucifixion . . . does the Word actually and wholly become flesh." Consequently, only in the Crucifixion does God die definitively to his original transcendent form.[24] In Altizer's view this is the only explanation which does full justice to the biblical meaning of divine *agape*. God would not have loved man with *agape,* i.e., he would not have given himself fully and totally to man if he had not emptied himself of his transcendent divine form of existence.

In Altizer's works, however, it never becomes clear whether the historical Jesus of Nazareth is a unique phenomenon in whom God *in his totality* has become man or whether he is only the beginning of a forward-moving *process* of Incarnation. At one point he insists: "what is new in the Christian name of Jesus is the epiphany of the totality of the sacred in the contingency of a particular moment of time."[25] But, more frequently, he stresses precisely the opposite: "A fundamental problem posed by the radical Christian vision of Christ is the concrete identity of the Incarnate Word. . . . the Word is not confined to the particular man, Jesus of Nazareth."[26]

So Altizer is more inclined to conceive of the existence and death of the historical Jesus as a mere starting point of a development in which the Word gradually becomes man. As a consequence, the death of God is also actualized gradually; it progresses in a movement parallel to that of universal incarnation. The process, however, went unnoticed for centuries. Only in the nineteenth century did the movement of "dying" take on more universal dimensions.[27] Its evident sign, which can no longer be ignored in our age, is that people and the-

---

[24]*Ibid.,* p. 54.

[25]*Ibid.,* p. 57.

[26]*Ibid.,* p. 71.

[27]At least this seems to me a probable interpretation of the ambiguous statement: "Although the death of God may not have been historically actualized or realized until the nineteenth century, the radical theologian cannot dissociate this event from Jesus and his original proclamation" ("Preface," *Radical Theology and the Death of God,* p. xii).

ologians find it increasingly more and more difficult to speak about God or believe in him.[28]

The eschatological end-point of the process is the totally Incarnate Word, "the Jesus who is actually and fully incarnate in every human hand and face."[29] The final coincidence of the opposites annihilates both God in his transcendence and the secular in its opposition to the sacred and realizes "the apocalyptic union of God and man." Altizer likes to describe this final stage with expressions taken from William Blake: the "One Man," "the New Jerusalem," "the universal Body of Jesus," or "the Great Humanity Divine."[30]

Already in *Mircea Eliade and the Dialectic of the Sacred,* but even more emphatically in *The Gospel of Christian Atheism* and *The New Apocalypse,* Altizer affirms the uniqueness of Christianity in contrast to any other religion, in particular to Oriental mysticism. The Eastern religions are characterized by a backward movement into a primordial Totality. The present world is simply and undialectically a negative and illusory reality of which one has to be freed in order to re-enter "the Beginning," "the sacred quiescent Reality."[31] Christianity alone knows about a forward-moving dialectic process in which the "Fall" from the Sacred Beginning is only one moment of the self-movement of God "becoming incarnate in the concrete contingency of time and space." So the future Eschaton is not a return to the beginning, but a new and final Paradise.[32]

Even though he emphasizes the unique character of Christianity, the nature of this final state remains closer to the Oriental vision, which believes in an ultimate identity of all things,

---

[28]See "Catholic Philosophy and the Death of God," *Cross Currents,* Summer, 1967, pp. 276-277.

[29]*The Gospel of Christian Atheism,* p. 71.

[30]See Thomas J. J. Altizer, *The New Apocalypse,* pp. 213-215, 218. In this last work, Altizer uses the word *eschatological* for the biblical view of the end, while to describe his own vision of the final state he employs the adjective *apocalyptic.* See *ibid.,* p. 215.

[31]*Ibid.,* p. 190.

[32]*Ibid.,* p. 192.

than to the Christian view of a personal union with God. "The Great Humanity Divine" is at once a "divine and human totality" where the selfhood of individual beings and the transcendent selfhood of God are definitively abolished.[33] For Altizer, personal selfhood seems identical to selfishness, an obstacle to real union. This is why the Kingdom where a new "Totality of Love" will be actualized demands the giving up of all personal distinction. In lieu of personal categories, Altizer presents it in terms of "flesh, body, energy," "ecstatic joy, bodily delight" and "fullness of life."[34] We come closer to "this apocalyptic consummation by every momentary death of Selfhood."[35]

The above picture of the final Paradise discloses, however, that the position of Altizer, though closer to Oriental religions than to Christianity, is still different from the former. While in Oriental mysticism all things are ultimately reduced to the Sacred, here the Sacred seems to be absorbed into the Secular. The third and final stage of the dialectic process, the coincidence of the Secular and the Sacred, is described in entirely Secular terms.

Jesus, in the first book of Altizer, was the most radical enemy of the world. But now he is identified with the Dionysius and the Zarathustra of Nietzsche, a radical yes-sayer to the world, to life, to the reality of the present moment.[36] He proclaims that true life, eternal life, is not a promise, not a future; "it is in

---

[33] See The Gospel of Christian Atheism, p. 131.

[34] See The New Apocalypse, p. 217; "The Waning Death of God Tumult," p. 18; The Gospel of Christian Atheism, p. 157.

[35] Obviously enough, in Altizer's vision there is no room for Resurrection and Ascension. A return to the transcendent realm is incompatible with his understanding of the Incarnation.

[36] It is worth noticing that the early Altizer supports his image of the world-denying Jesus by quoting the works of Nietzsche, and that the radical Altizer portrays the world-affirming Jesus according to the Nietzschean figure of Dionysius and Zarathustra. He also maintains that already Nietzsche has identified Jesus with the figure of Dionysius and Zarathustra. See Oriental Mysticism and Biblical Eschatology, p. 107; Mircea Eliade and the Dialectic of the Sacred, pp. 189-200; The Gospel of Christian Atheism, pp. 147-157.

you," here and now. The true glad tidings (precisely the opposite of the "ill-tidings" of the Christian Church) are "the blessedness of the present moment." The Jesus of the radical Christian accepts joyfully the Nietzschean "Eternal Recurrence" and welcomes "the eternal circular flux of being, being that begins again in every now."[37]

We cannot, however, enjoy the fullness of life (life understood in the sense of energy, of biological vitality[38]), we cannot participate unreservedly in the actuality of the present moment unless we are freed from the terror of guilt. To feel guilty, according to Altizer, is to refuse to live fully, because of the menacing, oppressing authority of a transcendent wholly other. Therefore, abolition of guilt, "forgiveness of sins," demands that God, the Holy Lord, be dead. If we believe in Altizer's Christ, we believe that God, the transcendent ground of the Law, has been forever abolished; hence, we are no longer under the Law, but free to live a new eschatological existence. What the free life, the total yes-saying to the world, means, whether it still implies certain moral standards which regulate human conduct, Altizer never makes clear. He mentions only "Love," a love abolishing all personal selfhood as the only cohesive force in the apocalyptic final state.[39]

Obviously enough, wherever Altizer presented his vision, he was confronted with the question: What is the reason on which his views are based? Is it a philosophical construction whose criterion is its rational demonstrability, or is it a vision of faith; and if the latter, what is its foundation?

If one inquires into the rational coherence of his thought on philosophical grounds, he evades the questioner by pointing out that his vision is a vision of Christian faith, understandable only to those who have faith. His faith, he insists, is very much in line with the purest eschatological and apocalyptic tradition

---

[37]*Mircea Eliade and the Dialectic of the Sacred*, p. 191.
[38]See the texts quoted under n. 34.
[39]*The Gospel of Christian Atheism*, pp. 128-157.

of the New Testament. In fact, what had been expected in the coming Kingdom at the time of Jesus was a "wholly new epiphany annihilating all that distance separating the creature from the Creator." But if one demonstrates to him that his faith is not the faith of the New Testament, he easily dismisses the objection as irrelevant: "There is no possibility of our returning to a primitive Christian faith." The Christ of the radical Christian is "neither the original historical Jesus, nor the Lord of the Church's earliest proclamation."[40] The decisive norm for the radical Christian is the revelation of the Spirit here and now. The revelation, however, on which the glad tidings of the death of God are based, has become possible only in our age, with the forward-moving process of Incarnation assuming more and more universal dimensions.[41]

In spite of this inconsistent fluctuation, Altizer maintains that his faith is the only possible alternative to unbelief for the contemporary man who does not want "to forfeit all the life and energy" of today's world.[42] In contemporary consciousness, the name of the transcendent God is unspeakable as a source of energy and life; transcendence appears to our consciousness as an empty, alien, lifeless form. And if God cannot be spoken of today as alive, he is truly and really dead. Thus the "faith" of Altizer in the death of God and in his new Christian gospel ultimately rests on a philosophical presupposition which he has never explicitly confronted: the existence of the transcendent God depends on man's consciousness of him; as long as man could conceive of him as a source of life and energy, he existed; as soon as man realized that transcendence can mean for him only alienation, repression, and negation of life, God died definitively as a transcendent Lord.[43]

Since Protestant reaction to Altizer's "New Christianity" has been by and large negative and quite often vehemently

---

[40]*Ibid.*, pp. 105-106.
[41]*Ibid.*, p. 27.
[42]*Ibid.*, p. 138.
[43]See "Catholic Philosophy and the Death of God," p. 281.

polemical, he has turned recently toward Catholic theology which, after Vatican II, especially in the United States, finds itself in a profound crisis of identity. He expressed his belief that Catholic theology has more chance to move, with "the least violent break with the past," toward an atheistic Christianity than any form of Protestantism. Protestantism is bound by the authority of the Bible and by the sixteenth-century dogmatics of the Reformers, while, according to him, Catholic theology is a "church theology" which "builds upon the Christian tradition in such a manner as to open the way to an evolutionary development which moves into the future by preserving but enlarging the forms of the past."[44] Since Catholic faith constantly develops and since God does not exist "independently of that which faith apprehends Him to be," we have to conclude that God himself moves through an evolutionary process.[45] This conclusion, according to Altizer, ought also to be drawn by Catholic theologians as a consequence of their much cherished doctrine of analogy. If there is an analogical relationship between the world and God, and if the world is seen today as moving and developing, it follows that the relationship between God and the world should be conceived of as "an evolving series of analogical relationships between the integrally related poles of a forward-moving process."[46]

How one must get by the "inherent" logic of Catholic theology from this Whiteheadian self-developing God to the death of God, Altizer does not explain. He merely quotes Teilhard de Chardin as the most radical of all Christian theologians whom he believes to be very close to his own position. In Altizer's interpretation, Teilhard would imply that "the evolution of consciousness is the evolution and involution of God himself"; at the final manifestation of the Omega point all distinctions between soul and nature, spirit and flesh, Christ and the world

---

[44]*Toward a New Christianity: Readings in the Death of God Theology* (New York: Harcourt, 1967), p. 2.
[45]"Catholic Philosophy and the Death of God," pp. 275-276.
[46]*Ibid.*, p. 273.

will collapse. God will be all in all in the sense that he "will be all in every consciousness, in every person, as finally the fullness of consciousness will reveal itself as being the fullness of God."[47] He does not seem to notice that even in the texts which he himself analyzes, Teilhard maintains the absolute transcendence of God as the sustaining Ground and final Goal of the cosmic evolution, but he himself not evolving. For Teilhard speaks of God as "the universal centre of unification [God in relation to the cosmos] (precisely to fulfill its motive, collective and stabilizing function), [he] must be conceived as pre-existing and transcendent." Nor does he pay attention to Teilhard's insistence that the "converging universe" is not born "from the fusion and confusion of the elemental centres it assembles." God being all in all does not abolish a real distinction between God and human persons on the one hand and among human centers of consciousness on the other. But God unites them to himself by the simultaneously "differentiating and communicating action of love."[48]

Besides the system of Teilhard, Altizer discovers motives for hope in the general christocentric tendency of contemporary Catholic theology, in its growing reluctance to speak about God apart from Christ and to speak about Christ apart from man.[49] He hopes, therefore, that Catholic theology will collapse into christology, and christology will be reduced to anthropology. While I deny that this insinuation does justice to modern Catholic theology in general, it has to be admitted, in my opinion, that he puts his finger on a widespread tendency in popularizing second-rate theological literature and on the practical religious attitude of many American Catholic intellectuals. Therefore his challenge deserves a serious reappraisal of where we are going in theology and why we are going in this direction.

---

[47]*Mircea Eliade and the Dialectic of the Sacred,* pp. 143, 148.

[48]*Ibid.,* p. 147, where Altizer quotes *The Phenomenon of Man* (New York: Harper & Row, 1959), p. 308.

[49]Altizer expressed these views in a seminar he conducted at the Catholic University in July, 1967.

To do this in detail and depth lies outside the scope of the present work. In the last chapter, however, I will attempt to draw an outline of the fundamental questions which should be examined in such a reconstruction of the theology of God.

4

PAUL M. VAN BUREN

Paul M. van Buren developed the most radical and the most consistent position among the death-of-God theologians. Although he never liked to be counted as one of the group or belonging to any "movement," he conceded in 1965 that Altizer and Hamilton agreed with him on one basic point: the question of God itself, "this whole manner of speaking about the category of the absolute—this has dissolved."[1] Beyond this common basis, he found more similarity between Hamilton and himself; this similarity lies in their background, "a background of study in Biblical theology, and therefore, broadly speaking, an interest in the historical, the human, the realm of the ethical."[2] But his interest in the pragmatic and ethical aspect of Christianity, his method of linguistic analysis based on empirical verification, have set up insurmountable barriers between him and the mystical vision and incoherent, exuberant language of Altizer. Besides, at a certain stage of his development, van Buren has drawn the final conclusions of his peculiar version of the "death of God" with more consistence than either Hamilton or Altizer. As van Buren has put it, in spite of

---

[1] Ved Mehta, *The New Theologian* (New York: Harper & Row, 1965), pp. 62-63. Paul M. van Buren is an ordained minister of the Episcopalian Church. He did graduate work at the Episcopal Theological School at Cambridge and at the University of Basel, where he received his doctorate in theology under K. Barth. Until the "death-of-God" controversy, he had been teaching at the Episcopal Theological Seminary of the Southwest, Austin, Texas. He is presently teaching at Temple University.

[2] *Ibid.*, p. 63.

his repeated affirmations that God is dead, at the end one is still not quite sure whether Hamilton means that God is only on vacation or that he will never return.[3] After he killed God, Altizer re-introduces him at the "apocalyptic" end when "God will be all in all." Although van Buren started out as a disciple of Barth (hence his original interest in christology and his aversion to natural theology), by 1965 he managed to get rid of the residue of a Christian vision more successfully than either of his two "colleagues." He came very close to the position of an atheistic humanist whose field of interest is exploring the possible meaning of the Western religious tradition (which *happens* to be Christian) for the contemporary secular man who finds belief in God completely meaningless. His theological career, from neoorthodoxy to a man-centered humanism, is perhaps the clearest example of how in our century Protestant neoorthodoxy produced neo-liberalism, as Protestant orthodoxy had developed liberal Protestantism in the nineteenth century. In spite of certain differences, a real parallel exists between the two movements. Both started with a one-sided emphasis on God's transcendence conceived as menacing terror and holiness for man; and both ended up with a one-sided emphasis on man even to the exclusion of God, a type of system best illustrated by that of Feuerbach in the nineteenth century, and by van Buren's secular interpretation of the Gospel in our age.

Yet, strangely enough, in his most recent articles, van Buren has moved away from this theological dead-end.[4] At least he may be said to put a question mark after everything he has written or started so far. In particular, he questions his own previous method of explaining the word *God* entirely in secular this-worldly terms (and thereby eliminating him from his system) and reopens the quest for God as the fundamental task

---

[3]*Ibid.*, p. 61.

[4]See Paul M. van Buren's latest book which is a collection of essays, *Theological Explorations* (New York: Macmillan, 1968), especially the "Introduction" and "Is Transcendence the Word We Want?"

of any theology, even in our secular age.

This movement of van Buren's thought will determine the structure of my study. First I will analyze his major work, *The Secular Interpretation of the Gospel,* published in 1963.[5] Though at first glance it appears to be a very systematic and coherent presentation, *The Secular Meaning of the Gospel* expresses a transitional stage in van Buren's thinking. Discarding any cognitive meaning of the word *God* he still hangs on to a christology as the final norm of ethical life. The second part of this chapter will try to summarize his articles written from 1964 through 1965, which will show how his thinking "has become a lot more radical."[6] Finally, I will attempt to analyze his last essays which reveal that he is far from being satisfied with the extreme conclusions of the death-of-God period; he even criticizes them and explores new avenues for the future of theology.

The purpose of *The Secular Meaning of the Gospel* is quite different from the intent of Altizer's or Hamilton's works. Van Buren is not concerned about making the Gospel acceptable to outsiders; he seeks the secular meaning of the Gospel for the contemporary secular man who is *within* the church.

First, he analyzes two contemporary interpretations of the Christian message in Protestant theology: the neoorthodox school of Karl Barth and the demythologizing movement of Rudolf Bultmann. Barth has rediscovered the central place of the Christ-event in Christian theology. This, for van Buren, is the great merit of the Barthian school. But he adds that the neoorthodox christology is sadly mythological in form and thus completely inaccessible to modern man.

Van Buren examines Bultmann's thought through the works of a Bultmann disciple, Schubert M. Ogden. He agrees with their fundamental concern to make the Gospel relevant and "unavoidable" for modern man by stripping it of its mythological form. Their conclusions, however, are, in his opinion,

---

[5]New York: Macmillan, 1963.
[6]Ved Mehta, *op. cit.,* p. 60.

untenable for two reasons. First, God, although through a new approach (as "the non-objective experienced reality" instead of the objective "thing" of classical theism), has still a central place in their system. God, whether in a neoclassical or classical approach, is simply unthinkable for modern man. Second, Bultmann and Ogden do not take seriously enough the historical basis of the Christian faith in Jesus of Nazareth. They replace it by Heidegger's philosophical analysis of existence.

Thus we are confronted by a dilemma: either we accept the christocentrism of the Gospel, following Barth, in which case our Christianity is mythological, inaccessible to secular man; or we accept the demythologizing method of Bultmann and Ogden, but then, logically, we have to reject the Christian Gospel itself. Moreover, even the position of Bultmann-Ogden is not sufficiently radical for contemporary man, since it preserves the idea of God.

Van Buren seeks to avoid the dilemma by using the philosophy of linguistic analysis. He recognizes that the approach of logical positivism, one of the main sources out of which the current method of language analysis has developed, is today inadequate. The logical positivists accept only two kinds of meaningful statements: assertions of mathematics and formal logic, and assertions about the physical world. The former are merely tautologies; they define our own terms in the way we are going to use them. Only the latter convey new information about reality, since they can be empirically verified. The logical meaning of a proposition about the physical world equals the sum of the sense-data by which it can be verified; e.g., the meaning of the statement "it rains" is obtained by observing and collecting all the sense-experiences which refer to it: e.g., you see clouds hanging in the sky, the pavement on the street is wet, if you go out of the house, you, too, will be wet, and so forth. It is evident that, in such a system, religious language is discarded as utterly meaningless.[7]

---

[7]See for more information the classic book by Alfred J. Ayer, *Language, Truth and Logic* (New York: Dover, 1952).

Van Buren agrees with the later Wittgenstein[8] and with most of today's language analysts that this system is arbitrarily limited. He is ready to acknowledge that there are as many different "language games" as there are diverse areas of modern life, politics, physics, esthetics, history. Each of the particular language games has its own rules, its own "logic," which can be applied only within that language game. It is obvious, e.g., that a statement like "I love you" has a meaning only within the context of human behavior. It would therefore be completely mistaken to interpret it by the criteria of scientific language. So in order to find out the meaning of a statement, one has to put it within the context of the language game to which it belongs and to examine its function or use within that language. Its meaning will be found in, and will be identical with, the function of the statement.

But in order to decide whether or not a statement has a function and to determine what its function is, one has to weigh carefully what empirical evidence counts for or against that statement. At this point, however, it becomes clear that, although van Buren explicitly rejects the principle of empirical verification of logical positivism, he re-introduces it in a slightly modified form under the guise of language analysis. His criterion of meaning is ultimately still that of empirical evidence, albeit it is no longer restricted to physical experience, but accepts also "ordinary human experiences" such as those pertaining to love, service, freedom, moral commitments. But he excludes the possibility of a specific religious experience which would refer to God, a transcendent reality inaccessible to the senses. He provides both philosophical and theological grounds for the exclusion.

The famous parable of Anthony Flew serves as a basis for the philosophical reasoning:

Once upon a time two explorers came upon a clearing in the

---

[8]See Ludwig Wittgenstein, *Philosophical Investigations* (Oxford: Blackwell, 1953).

jungle. In the clearing were growing many flowers and many weeds. One explorer says, "Some gardener must tend this plot." The other disagrees. "There is no gardener." So they pitch their tents and set a watch. No gardener is ever seen. "But perhaps it is an invisible gardener." So they set up a barbed wire fence. They electrify it. They patrol with bloodhounds. . . . But no shrieks ever suggest that some intruder has received a shock. No movement of the wire ever betrays an invisible climber. The bloodhounds never give cry. Yet still the Believer is not convinced. "But there is a gardener, invisible, intangible, insensible to electric shocks, a gardener who has no scent and makes no sound, a gardener who comes secretly to look after the garden which he loves." At last the Skeptic despairs, "But what is left of your original assertion? Just how does what you call an invisible, intangible, eternally elusive gardener differ from an imaginary gardener or even from no gardener at all?" [Flew concludes:] A fine brash hypothesis may thus be killed by inches, the death of a thousand qualifications.[9]

So it is with the statement "God exists." Since no empirical evidence can ever be brought up which could falsify it, the proposition is simply meaningless. In other words, one cannot say that the course of history, or the state of the world, would in any way be different if God did not exist. But an assertion which is compatible with anything or everything, says nothing. Consequently, the word *God* dies the death of a thousand qualifications; it is a "dead word," and has no meaning whatsoever. This is, in a short summary, the philosophical reasoning on the basis of which van Buren chooses to deny any cognitive content to God-statements.

Another ground, however, and in van Buren's view, a more important one is, quite surprisingly, a theological consideration:

We reject the cognitive approach to theological language, however, not primarily because it is logically puzzling, but because of certain theological commitments out of which this study has arisen. That approach builds its case on a natural sense of the divine, on natural religion and a natural revelation. The history

---

[9]Paul M. van Buren, *The Secular Meaning of the Gospel,* p. 3.

of theology, seen from the perspective of modern kerygmatic theology, suggests that this is a road leading into the wilderness. Within the Protestant tradition, the road has been clearly charted and firmly marked with a "dead-end" sign by the work of Karl Barth, and we see no reason to ignore the warning.[10]

Thus God-statements *cannot* have any reference to God, whether understood as the "objective Super-Being" of what van Buren calls "literal theism" or conceived of as "the non-objective experienced reality" of Ogden's "qualified theism." Nevertheless, van Buren does not intend to dismiss the whole language of Christian faith as totally meaningless. On the contrary, his purpose is to make Christian faith relevant to the empirically minded secular Christian. Here we come across the basic contradiction of his enterprise: his avowed aim is to conduct a conversation "from faith to faith," i.e., to seek the meaning of faith for believers. But in reality, he attempts to reduce Christian faith, which, by its very nature, claims to transcend the realm of sense experience, to what is empirically verifiable. Before he spells out his own position, he evaluates several contemporary approaches to religious language.

The theory of R. M. Hare about the "blik" is proposed with particular sympathy. The "blik" will become one of the cornerstones of van Buren's own interpretation.[11] According to Hare, each of us has a "blik," i.e., certain fundamental attitudes which are empirically unverifiable, and "yet everything we do depends on them." The mistake of the skeptic in Flew's parable was that he took the Believer's words about the gardener for an explanation of how things are in reality, while it was only the expression of his particular "blik": "an orientation, a commitment to see the world in a certain way and a way of life following inevitably upon this orientation."[12] A student

---

[10] *Ibid.*, p. 98.
[11] "Here I present van Buren's understanding of Hare's "blik." I do not concern myself with the problem as to what extent van Buren's interpretation does justice to Hare's theory.
[12] *Ibid.*, p. 87.

may have the insane "blik" that every don is persecuting him; and regardless of any empirical evidence to the contrary, he will stubbornly stick to his "blik." But not only the insane student! Everyone has a "blik"; just one is sane, the other is insane. There is, of course, no valid criterion to distinguish between the two, since a "blik" is not an explanation that can be proved true or false. In Hare's opinion, and van Buren heartily agrees with him, Christian faith should be understood as a particular "blik."

Another philosopher from whom van Buren borrows some elements for his own theory is Ian T. Ramsey. Statements of faith, Ramsey points out, refer to a certain kind of situation, to "situations of disclosure." The function of religious language is to direct our attention to such situations, although it cannot, by itself, bring about such situations. But using "models," i.e., words which derive from experience and point in a certain direction (e.g., "father") and adding "qualifiers" to them (e.g., eternal, omnipotent, all-good), we can "stretch" their meaning until "the light dawns." Then we discern a depth, a mystery; i.e., we encounter Someone who is beyond ordinary human experience and to whom we cannot assign a name, but he reveals to us his name. The odd word *God* stands for the ineffable name which was given to us in a "situation of disclosure." The discernment we thus received is inseparable from a response commitment which gives a definite direction to our whole life.

Van Buren takes over the terms *discernment* and *commitment* from Ramsey, but does not pay any attention to the cognitive character of discernment in Ramsey's theory. For Ramsey, the statements of Christian faith describe a disclosure situation whose occasion and object is Jesus Christ, in whom the transcendent objective love of God is truly present and revealed.[13]

Another linguistic analyst who strongly influences van

[13]See, e.g., Ian T. Ramsey, "Discernment, Commitment and Cosmic Disclosure," *Religious Education,* January-February, 1965, pp. 10-14.

Buren's approach is R. B. Braithwaite. For Braithwaite "religious assertions are in fact *used as* moral assertions."[14] They express the intention of the assenter to act in a way specified in the assertion. Religious assertions, however, are distinct from purely moral assertions because a Christian declares his intention to behave in a certain way *in connection* with the Christian story. Whether or not the story corresponds to historical facts is irrelevant. Van Buren basically agrees with Braithwaite, although in *The Secular Meaning of the Gospel* he attributes more weight to the historical foundations of the Christian faith, in particular, to the Easter event, than Braithwaite would admit. In his later articles of '64 and '65, however, he accepts the term *Christian story* in the same ahistorical sense as Braithwaite does.

These three philosophers, Hare, Ramsey (in a distorted form), and Braithwaite, provide the immediate bases for van Buren's interpretation of religious talk which can be summed up in the following points.

1. Theism, either in its "literal" or "qualified" form, is dead.

2. Yet faith-statements do have a meaning. They must be interpreted according to the modified verification principle exhaustively and without remainder as man-statements; they express, describe, or suggest a particular way of seeing the world, other men, and one's self, and a way of life appropriate to such perspective.

3. "The norm of the Christian perspective is the series of events to which the New Testament documents testify, centering in the life, death, and resurrection of Jesus of Nazareth."[15]

4. How the Christian perspective becomes normative for one is explained by Hare's theory of "blik." The Believer "has been caught" by the Gospel; he "has been grasped and held."

---

[14]See *The Secular Meaning of the Gospel*, p. 93, quoting R. B. Braithwaite, *An Empiricist's View of Religious Belief* (Cambridge: Cambridge University Press, 1955), p. 11.

[15]*The Secular Meaning of the Gospel*, p. 156.

Faith in Jesus is "given," "the believer cannot and does not want to take any credit for it."[16]

The "blik" theory stands out as a foreign body in the system of van Buren based on secular empirical presuppositions. What does he mean when he uses the passive voice: to be caught, to be grasped? He recognizes that no "blik" can be empirically verified. Is then the Christian "blik" a merely arbitrary option for man or is it the last remainder of the doctrine of grace? But then whose grace does he talk about if "God" is to be discarded definitively? In any case, the "blik" theory as applied to Christianity is incompatible with the sober empirical attitude of modern man as defined by van Buren.[17]

The most original contribution of van Buren is his reinterpretation of christology in the light of the above-mentioned philosophical presuppositions. The method is relatively simple: he applies the modified verification principle to the christological statements of the New Testament and thereby establishes their meaning. It is instructive to see how the method works on some concrete examples.

Van Buren readily admits that the basic characteristic of Jesus in the Gospels is his trust and faith in God the Father whom he worships and obeys, and who reveals him as his Son. But all this is subjected to empirical verification: "We have no idea what would count for or against the assertion that in seeing Jesus one had seen the Father."[18] What modern man can grasp, since it can be part of his ordinary experience and he knows what would count for, or against, it, is the astonishing freedom of Jesus: freedom from family ties, from fear, from any urge to establish his identity. But his real greatness lies in his freedom for others; he dedicated his whole life to serve them. Thus, what is empirically verifiable of the faith of Jesus is his freedom.

[16]*Ibid.*, p. 140.
[17]See John Macquarrie, *God and Secularity* (Philadelphia: Westminster, 1967), p. 22.
[18]*The Secular Meaning of the Gospel*, p. 147.

For van Buren, therefore, the freedom of Jesus is not just the consequence of his faith, it *is* its logical meaning.

The resurrection has to be understood in a similar way. Concerning the rising of Jesus to a new "eschatological life," the only experience which is subject to our control is a radical change in the behavior of the Apostles: fearful and insecure before, they begin to act with the very freedom of Jesus. Whatever may have happened between the death of Jesus and this radical transformation of the disciples cannot be verified. The only fact open to historical investigation is that the freedom of Jesus "became contagious" on Easter Sunday. Consequently, this is the logical meaning of the resurrection.

At this point we are again tempted to ask: What is the meaning of the metaphor: "the freedom of Jesus began to be contagious"? Does it refer to an "ordinary human experience," in the manner in which a smile is contagious or a fear can become contagious and produce panic? Some expressions van Buren uses do not fit in this pattern, e.g., "the light dawned" or Jesus is the "liberator" in whose freedom the disciples share, "not by their own choice," but "as something which happens" to them.[19] Thus, "one cannot help wondering, whether . . . van Buren is not breaking out [again] from the self-imposed limits of his 'reduced' theology . . . he seems to be speaking of something very like what is traditionally called 'grace.' "[20]

The idea of freedom understood in the general humanistic sense as freedom for the service of others is central to the reinterpretation of the whole Gospel. "The Gospel . . . is not merely about a free man: it is the good news of a free man who has set other men free."[21] This is the meaning of the proclamation of the Early Church: "Jesus is Lord."

The history of Jesus as a free man is the *exclusive* norm in the light of which the Christian is to interpret himself, other men,

---

[19]*Ibid.*, p. 133.
[20]See n. 17.
[21]*Ibid.*, p. 138.

and the whole world. The history of Jesus is also *a universal* norm for "the believer." "He understands all free men, regardless of where they may say they have found their freedom, as having 'caught' their freedom from the same source as he." It is also a *final* norm for the Christian. All other loyalties, loyalty to his nation, Church, family, or any other person, are relative to, and consequent upon, his primary allegiance to Jesus. In fact, this absolute commitment to Christ liberates him "for service to these other centers of relative loyalty."[22]

Van Buren finds a way also to give a meaning to the traditional formula that "Jesus is God" without reference to a transcendent God who would have become incarnate in Jesus. He contends that the New Testament itself points out the way for his interpretation. Since Jesus is the only and adequate revelation of the Father, and "there is no 'Father' to be found apart from him and since his 'Father' can only be found in him, the New Testament gives its answer to the question about 'God' by pointing to the man Jesus." So the logical meaning of the formula "Jesus is God" can only be: "whatever men were looking for in 'God' is to be found by finding Jesus of Nazareth."[23]

Even prayer itself finds a place in van Buren's reconstruction of Christianity. Relying again on the principle that the meaning of a word is its reference to an empirically verifiable experience, he concludes that the meaning of prayer is the readiness of the Christian to help his neighbor. In ancient times, the Christian helped his neighbor in the best way he could; in case of aridity, for instance, he prayed to God for rain. Today, his actions will be different:

> Although he will be doing the same thing: he will reflect on his neighbor's plight in the light of the Gospel . . . He has been set free from self-concern in order to be concerned for his neighbor. He will therefore set about doing just what ancient man was

[22]*Ibid.*, p. 142.
[23]*Ibid.*, p. 147.

doing: the most effective thing he knows of to relieve his neighbor's distress . . . he will go to see his neighbor, study the situation with him, and see what can be done to get water on the
fields by irrigation or other means.[24]

In his later articles van Buren admits that in reconstructing
the New Testament message he not only applied a new
method (that of linguistic analysis), but presupposed a certain
metaphysics: the common sense metaphysics of today's secular man: "the kinds of responses which we take to be answers
to our question, as opposed to those which strike us as eva-
sions or nonsense, reveal our operative understandings of the
way things are, of what is 'real' and what matters to us."[25]

He never defines clearly this "network of operative understandings," but its fundamental assumption is evident to anyone who has read carefully *The Secular Meaning of the Gospel*:
reality is limited to what can (in some loose sense) be empirically verified. Van Buren intends to use his metaphysics
merely as a "descriptive," not as a "normative" one; i.e.,
theoretically, he does not claim that his metaphysics is true:
"that the patterns and presuppositions of our daily thinking
ought to be what they seem to be, is not a question I have
argued."[26] He is merely interested in seeing what kind of theology could be constructed on such grounds.

In practice, however, van Buren could not avoid presuppos-
ing the universal validity of his metaphysical outlook. In *The
Secular Meaning of the Gospel* he claims that, although he
uses a new language and transforms the assertions of the
apostolic message and the faith of the Fathers into historical
and ethical statements, he remains faithful to the "intention"
of the New Testament and of its patristic interpretation. He
believes that he "left nothing essential behind" and transmitted

[24]*Ibid.*, pp. 188-189.
[25]"Christian Education in a Pragmatic Age," *Theological Explorations*,
pp. 63-64.
[26]*Ibid.*, p. 64.

for secular Christianity "the full tradition of the faith."[27] He even maintains that his reappraisal of the Christian faith has the same meaning as the faith of orthodox Christianity. Of course, in ancient times "God was part of what people took to be the network of forces and factors of everyday existence, as real and as objective as the thunderbolts he produced."[28] This is why at that time God as an object was part of the Christian faith. At this point, it becomes evident that van Buren projects his own metaphysics into the time of Early Christianity, and thus considers it as normative. He cannot accept any understanding of God but a crudely empirical one: God as one of the particular objects of this world. He does not even allow the possibility that some philosophers or theologians *could* mean by God a transcendent Being qualitatively different from our world.

Moreover, when equating the meaning of his christology with that of orthodox christology, he tacitly implies that christological statements can mean *only* what he means by them, i.e., they all refer to the man Jesus as the paradigm and "virus-carrier" of human freedom.[29] Once again, his metaphysical presupposition becomes absolutely normative. Otherwise he could not claim an identity of meaning, as he consistently does through *The Secular Meaning of the Gospel.*

After 1963, van Buren's position became even more radical. By 1964 he had gradually dismissed all the remnants of his Barthian heritage. He no longer taught at the Episcopal Theological Seminary of the Southwest, but transferred to the department of religion in a "large secular urban university." He regards this move as symbolic. In 1963, he still considered theology as a "church discipline" and, as we have seen, made painstaking efforts to prove that his secular interpretation is

---

[27]*The Secular Meaning of the Gospel,* p. 200.
[28]"The Dissolution of the Absolute," *Theological Explorations,* p. 36.
[29]Cf. J. Robert Nelson, "Deicide, Theothanasia, or What Do You Mean," *The Meaning of the Death of God,* ed. by Bernard Murchland (New York: Random, Vintage Books, 1967), p. 201.

faithful to traditional Christianity.[30] In 1964, he was no longer bothered by such concerns. He became convinced that theology or religious thought is not responsible to the Church, but to human society. Religious studies are a division of the humanities. Their function is to provide "an accompaniment" to the "main melody" of human culture. Neoorthodox theology refused to take part in the concert "and went off into a corner to practice a more ancient melody." But modern theology has to take up the role it has played before Barth. Once again, theology must become an integral, though subordinate, part of human culture. In terms of the above-mentioned metaphor this will mean that it must "pick up the score as it was being played some decades ago and see if we can catch up with the development of the main melody, changing key, even changing formal structure, with the hope of adding an accompaniment which might help round out a score that seems at times a bit hollow."[31]

The radical van Buren of '64 adopted Braithwaite's term *Christian story*; this he had refused to do in '63. He became much less concerned about "the empirical footing" of the Christian story in actual history. His Christianity was concerned more and more unambiguously "about man and human life and human history"—about "a certain form of life—patterns of human existence, norms of human attitudes . . . and moral behavior." The study of this humanism and its development in Western civilization, became the central issues for him; "whether and to what extent this humanism was influenced by Christianity"—he admitted frankly in 1964—is for him "a secondary question."[32]

By analyzing the ideas of van Buren's articles written around 1964, one could reasonably have come to the conclusion that he has consistently drawn all the consequences of his position as outlined in *The Secular Meaning of the Gospel* and has finally

---

[30]*The Secular Meaning of the Gospel*, p. 158.
[31]"Theology in the Context of Culture," *Frontline Theology*, p. 49.
[32]Ved Mehta, *op. cit.*, p. 66.

settled down as an atheistic humanist. This would, however, grossly distort the facts. In 1964, van Buren was far from reaching a fixed and stable stand. As early as 1965, we can discern a certain "loosening up" in his articles. He likes to think that "at least in some of these [new] essays" he has overcome "a certain 'muscle-bound' quality" of his last book, *The Secular Meaning of the Gospel*.[33] Under the continuing influence of the later Wittgenstein, through the discovery of William James and John Wisdom, he returns again and again from various points of departure to the same problems which he seemed to have definitively settled in his previous studies. He does not recapture the christological concern of his Barthian period. But he questions as too simplistic, "too prosaic and too unimaginative" all the answers he previously gave to theological problems.[34]

It would go counter to the explicit intention of van Buren if one tried to identify this new "position" on the basis of his newest writings; he insists that his present position is not to have any "frozen position" at all. Every essay represents only "one frame of a moving picture film" which has been taken of a dancer. As in the case of a dancer, not the individual postures, but "the movement of the dance itself" is important. Therefore we should look for a certain movement in his thought rather than for a fixed system.[35] The "movement" which, in van Buren's view, is essentially open-ended and provisional, can perhaps best be described by the following characteristics.

1. Through his continuous study of language analysis, he discovered that not everything which has to be said can be said "clearly and neatly," but poetry, images, and metaphors have an important role to play in human language. He truly acknowledges now the diversity of different language games and no longer adheres to a rigid principle of empirical verifi-

---

[33]"Introduction," *Theological Explorations*, p. 5.
[34]"Is Transcendence the Word We Want?" *Theological Explorations*, pp. 180-181.
[35]See n. 33.

ability. Therefore, Braithwaite's categorization of religious statements is rejected as inadequate. For, as he says:

> Religious statements become, in this treatment, just as clear as the classes with which Braithwaite began, as clear and as flat. If one is left with a sense that this interesting argument has not done justice to the subject, the fault may be assigned to the point of departure rather than to the resultant analysis of the function of religious language. If one wishes above all else to be factual and clear, one will hunt far to find a better answer than that provided by Braithwaite to the question of what religion is.[36]

2. The "God question" which was apparently taken care of with such ease and elegance in *The Secular Meaning of the Gospel* comes to the foreground again. He is convinced now that the question of God, as a problem which does not admit of clear and simple answers, is even today an important theological issue. By criticizing the method of G. Kaufman, who tried to "translate 'God' into the language of 'this-worldly' (i.e., 'secular') experiences and conceptions," he implicitly condemns the approach of his own previous book.[37] Such an effort of "translation" is as difficult as "trying to translate the language of love into the language of biology."

3. Besides, why should the word *God* be translated at all? It belongs to a specific language game, the religious language which corresponds to a specific and irreducible experience: it has to be investigated on its own grounds. Rather than a sense of limitation, as suggested by Kaufman (van Buren does not exclude his approach, but finds it inadequate), he proposes "a sense of wonder" as a point of departure for understanding religious language. Van Buren contends that this experience cannot be written off as obsolete merely because "modern theologians" lack such experience. He believes that true religious experience was and *is* even today the privilege of a "few and strange" people:

---

[36]"Introduction," *Theological Explorations,* p. 8.
[37]"Is Transcendence the Word We Want?" p. 164.

Speech about God, or silence about God, for that matter, but in any case, the sort of speech and the sort of silence that marks off the strange ones from the masses, the deep ones from the superficial, appears within the context of a sense of wonder, awe and joy before what is there for all to behold; the fact that we are alive, that there is anything at all. The mystical, as Wittgenstein put it, and he was surely one of the strange ones, is not how the world is, but *that* it is. This sense of awe and wonder occurs when one is *struck* by the fact that I am, and that I am I, that a tree is itself, that there is anything at all, in short when all these things, oddly enough, no longer seem to be self-evident to us and no cause for surprise.

This experience was called by the ancients: trembling in the presence of God or gods. But whether one uses the word *God* or not, is irrelevant. The decisive point to be made is that some people "are *struck* by the ordinary, whereas most find it only ordinary."[38]

4. While reflecting on what it means that some people are struck by the ordinary *as* extraordinary, he discovers more and more "the metaphysical character of theology."[39] He is confronted with what he calls "the central problem for theology today": the metaphysical task of justifying a certain religious "way of seeing," a "perspective" for which, beforehand, he had used the word "blik." But he no longer employs this term, since he realizes now that adopting a certain perspective is not an entirely neutral and unexplainable matter: "We do not want to say . . . that since everyone has some perspective, anyone may have whatever perspective he wants."[40] He sees clearly, at least in some cases (Hitler and Lee Oswald), that one perspective is to be preferred to the other. He also knows that " 'we have grounds' for seeing things as we do."[41] He had come a long way from the concept of "blik" in which there was no valid ground to distinguish between a sane and an insane

---

[38]*Ibid.*, pp. 169-170.
[39]"Introduction," *Theological Explorations*, p. 4.
[40]"Is Transcendence the Word We Want?" p. 172.
[41]*Ibid.*, p. 173.

"blik," to conceding that there are grounds for adopting a definite metaphysical (and religious) perspective. He admits that he is not at all clear about what these grounds are and what the process of justifying our views might mean. Yet van Buren is far from giving up the search. The amazing intellectual honesty and courage which enabled him to put a question mark after almost everything he had written before may still lead him to unpredictable new discoveries.[42]

---

[42]I did not analyze his essay "William James and the Metaphysical Risk," *Theological Explorations,* pp. 135-160, because whatever he says about God (the limited God as a possible hypothesis who can also become the ultimate end of our life) seems to represent James' thought rather than his own.

THEOLOGICAL
BACKGROUND

5

RUDOLF BULTMANN

After one has examined the position of each of the three radical theologians, it remains to be seen how much their thought has been influenced by crisis theology and neo-orthodoxy. They themselves admit this influence. In particular, they refer to Rudolf Bultmann, to Paul Tillich, to the early Barth, and to the two posthumous works of Dietrich Bonhoeffer. To state such connections may seem, at first glance, puzzling, since Bultmann, Tillich, Barth, and Bonhoeffer built up their theology in conscious opposition to the theological reductionism of the nineteenth-century liberal Protestant theology. The death-of-God trend is certainly closer in its final conclusions to nineteenth-century liberalism than to neo-orthodoxy or crisis theology. A deeper study, however, will disclose, I believe, an intrinsic link between the thought of the "Big Four" and radical theology. It will be my task in the following part of this work to bring to light the strange logic inherent in the works of Bultmann, Tillich, Barth, and Bonhoeffer, which, contrary to the intentions of the authors, has led to the re-emergence of a reductionist theology.

Bultmann is deeply concerned about safeguarding the transcendence of the Word of God. As a reaction against Schleiermacher, he never ceases to stress that the Word of God cannot be reduced to a datum of our religious consciousness.[1]

---

[1] F. Schleiermacher was one of the greatest representatives of liberal Protestant theology in the nineteenth century.

It comes from the outside; man can never get hold of it. It confronts man in the actual preaching of the Church; it passes judgment over him and impels him to decide for or against it. The Word of God cannot be identified with any objective content, with a revelation of divine mysteries. It is essentially an act of God, an address to me here and now that calls from death to life, from unfaith to faith.[2]

Even though he is preoccupied with revitalizing a theology of the Word of God, Bultmann remains deeply indebted to the methods and presuppositions of liberal theology. In particular, he accepts and develops the conclusions of the school of the history of religions.[3] Comparing the New Testament material with the mythologies of ancient religions contemporary to the New Testament period, he finds far-reaching structural identities. He admits, however, a certain difference, namely, the presence of a historical core behind and within the Christian myth. But according to him this historical core cannot be recaptured by us. He believes that the historical figure and the historical event of Jesus of Nazareth was soon transformed into a myth by the creative imagination of the primitive Church. Thus, the pre-existent Son of God was born of a virgin by the miraculous intervention of the Holy Spirit; he walked around performing miracles; he sacrificed himself on the cross, thereby placating God's wrath through his own blood for the sins of a fallen humanity. He rose from the dead, ascended into heaven, and will soon come to judge the world in an apocalyptic catastrophe. Then redeemed man will be transferred into a celestial realm of light and endowed with a spiritual body.[4] All these elements

[2]See, e.g., R. Bultmann, "The Concept of Revelation in the New Testament," *Existence and Faith,* translated and introduced by S. M. Ogden (New York: Meridian, 1960), pp. 87-88.

[3]The main representatives of this school are W. Bousset and W. Heitmüller.

[4]See, e.g., "New Testament and Mythology," *Kerygma and Myth, A Theological Debate,* ed. by H. W. Bartsch, revised edition of the translation by R. H. Fuller (New York: Harper & Row, 1966), p. 2. This essay was delivered by Bultmann in 1943 and started the debate on demythologization.

were borrowed, according to Bultmann, from "Jewish apocalyptic and Gnostic redemption myths."[5] He does not bother
too much to explain what he understands by myth. It is only
in one of the footnotes of his famous essay "New Testament and Mythology" that he gives a rather loose and ambiguous
definition of myth: "Mythology is the use of imagery to express
the other worldly in terms of this world and the divine in terms
of human life, the other side in terms of this side."[6] Bultmann
states that for modern man, whose thinking is "shaped for good
or ill by modern science," mythological language is "not only
irrational, but utterly meaningless."[7]

Does this mean that the New Testament as a whole has to be
discarded? By no means! Bultmann's purpose is not to throw
out the New Testament mythology, but to find its true meaning, the *kerygma* (message) which is both expressed and ob-
scured by what he considers the outdated mythological
language. The only solution to this hermeneutical problem is,
in Bultmann's view, an existentialist re-interpretation. His idea
is that the Christian myth, in a time-conditioned, clumsy, ob-
jectified way, intends to express an existential encounter of
man with the Word of God "in the reality of his personal life
and in his transformation."[8] Therefore, to restate the New
Testament message in an understandable language, one has to
use the categories of contemporary existentialist philosophy,
in particular those of Heidegger's existentialist analysis. Thus
the judgment of God's Word over me is presented as a bringing to light, and a condemnation of my previous inauthentic
existence, which was a "life according to the flesh" in Paul's
words, an anxious and desperate clinging to visible, this-worldly
passing securities. At the same time, however, God's Word
graciously offers me the realization of a new authentic self-

---

[5]*Ibid.*, p. 15.
[6]*Ibid.*, p. 10.
[7]*Ibid.*, p. 8.
[8]*Ibid.*

understanding, a "life according to the spirit" in Pauline terms, enabling me to be liberated from the ties of my past life and to accept my future in an unconditional surrender to God.

Bultmann is convinced that such interpretation corresponds to the deepest intention of the New Testament writers. In fact, he thinks that the process of demythologization was started by St. Paul and St. John. John, according to Bultmann, discarded the crude apocalyptic eschatology of the primitive community in which the *eschaton* meant a temporal and objective event to be expected in the imminent future. For John the eschatological event is understood as an existential one. Every moment can become an eschatological moment, i.e., eschatology takes place whenever and wherever man is confronted with the Word of God and passes over from death to life, or in Heideggerian terms, from inauthentic to authentic existence.

Likewise, St. Paul gives an existential dimension to the crucifixion and resurrection of Christ. He still believes in miracles, like all his contemporaries. Yet for Paul, Bultmann contends, the cross and resurrection mean primarily a dying and rising of the believer, i.e., rising to a new existential self-understanding, as expressed in John's Gospel. To be sure, Bultmann does not intend to eliminate the Easter event. On the contrary, he believes that he has uncovered its real meaning. The resurrection is an act of God, but it is an act of God only *in the believer*.

The underlying presupposition of reducing faith to an existential encounter is, I believe, a threefold one:

1. Bultmann inherited a Kantian epistemology. Thus for him any metaphysical "objective" knowledge of God is impossible. God as an object of human thinking would be a creation of human thinking, an idol in the eyes of the Protestant Bultmann. God can be known only in the act of his self-revelation, but even then what one knows is only the human subject affected by God's revealing Word.[9]

---

[9]Cf. "What Sense Is There in Talking of God," transl. in *The Christian Scholar*, XXXXIII, 213-222.

2. A miraculous intervention of God in the objective outside world is inconceivable for modern man: the world is a close weft of causes and effects. Consequently, "a corpse cannot leave the tomb": the bodily resurrection of Jesus is nonsense.[10]

3. Not only modern scientific thinking, but also the correct understanding of God's absolute transcendence excludes such intervention. The divine cannot be expressed in the terms of this world; therefore the Incarnation, in the traditional sense of God *becoming man*, is excluded by God's infinite otherness. God intervenes only in my personal life as a Word addressed to me here and now at a quasi-mathematical point of my historical existence; it is always an event, a transition, so that I can see only God's "back."[11]

Some critics of Bultmann object that he has not followed his own program of demythologization to its logical conclusions. If it is historically unverifiable and theologically irrelevant who Jesus was and what he preached and did, why should we then link the present event of acquiring a new self-understanding to the event of Jesus of Nazareth? Bultmann argues desperately (in spite of the logic of his system, I believe, but in this insistence, he shows that he wants to remain a Christian) that, regardless of the "what-ness" of the Jesus event, its mere fact is connected with the present Word event. It is the Word of *Christ* that confronts me here and now.[12]

Other critics, e.g., van Buren, as we have seen before, object that a consistent demythologization should have eliminated the idea of God altogether. It is as meaningless to contemporary man as the rest of the mythological imagery. If we accept the premises of Bultmann that myth is the expression of the other-worldly in terms of this world and agree that all that is myth-

---

[10] See the interview with the retired Bultmann, "Spiegel Gespräch mit dem Marburger Theologieprofessor D. Dr. Rudolf Bultmann," *Der Spiegel,* July 25, 1966, p. 45.

[11] Cf. René Marlé, *Bultmann et l'interprétation du Nouveau Testament,* revised ed. (Paris: Aubier, 1966), pp. 181-208.

[12] One of these critics in Germany is F. Buri.

ological has to be interpreted as talk about human existence, we must agree that there are no grounds whatsoever to make an exception for the "act of God." If all the "supernatural entities" and powers, like "Pneuma," Satan, and angels, can be explained as immanent factors of human existence, why should "God" not be reduced to one of these? Moreover, if the so-called secular man cannot accept the intervention of God into the objective world of nature, why is it easier for him to accept such intervention into his own personal life?[13] Bultmann struggles with this difficulty. His only answer is that an act of God in one's personal existence is not a mythological, but an analogical, expression understood according to the analogy of human personal encounter.[14] This, however, within the framework of Bultmann's system, remains an unfounded assertion, inconsistent with his program of demythologization.

This short analysis of Bultmann's understanding of God discloses a striking paradox. The one-sided insistence of Bultmann on the absolute transcendence of God who cannot be known as an object of philosophical investigation, who cannot become man without compromising his divine holiness, leads logically to the opposite extreme of immanentism. If God is only a factor in existential experience, if "the question of God and the question of myself are identical,"[15] then we had better stop talking about God altogether. Then van Buren's conclusion is right, although it runs contrary to the intention of Bultmann:

> If in the language of faith a statement about God is really a statement about man . . . then to say that this is equally language about "God and his activities" is to assert that the same words refer to man, where they are verifiable, and to God, where they are not. That is confusing, to say the least. If "God loves me"

---

[13]My criticism concerning this point is based on J. Macquarrie, *God-Talk: An Examination of the Language and Logic of Theology* (London: SCM, 1967), pp. 36-39.

[14]*Jesus Christ and Mythology* (New York: Scribner's, 1958), p. 68.

[15]*Ibid.*, p. 53.

means, "I feel secure, wanted, of value," then the second sentence can function perfectly well in place of the first. It does not follow, however, that "God loves me" will function in the place of "I feel secure" . . . One statement cannot be "cashed" (i.e., it cannot be subjected to empirical verification): the other can. They are not the same, therefore, and if we insist on saying that one will function in place of the other and vice versa, then we have arrived at the place where muddle masquerades as mystery.[16]

Altizer considers Bultmann as one of the important sources for radical theology. He quotes those passages from Bultmann's *Theology of the New Testament* which insist that Jesus as the final Word of God does not reveal anything about God, except that Jesus as man is the Revealer. Revelation cannot mean any knowledge of God, according to Bultmann; it merely conveys the power of transforming one's existence. Thus, Altizer believes that Bultmann's theology also bears witness to the central argument on which Altizer's position is based: contemporary man can no longer speak about God; as a consequence, he cannot believe in him; therefore God must be dead.[17]

---

[16]*The Secular Meaning of the Gospel,* pp. 67-88.
[17]See *Towards a New Christianity,* ed. by T. J. J. Altizer, pp. 177-198.

6

PAUL TILLICH

While Bultmann is primarily a biblical scholar who interprets the results of his exegesis in the light of a Heideggerian existentialism, Tillich builds up a monumental synthesis of systematic theology, although he himself starts with an analysis of human existence. The whole of Tillich's thought cannot be treated here. The scope of this study is restricted to Tillich's understanding of God (of course, this can be done only within the context of the whole of his theology), in the light of which I shall attempt to establish whether the radical theologians are justified in claiming Tillich as one of the major sources of their theology.

A first glance at the conflicting evaluations of Tillich's doctrine of God shows that the complexity of his thought admits of contradictory interpretations. According to C. Kiesling, the basic problem in interpreting Tillich's idea of God is his new and disconcerting terminology. Once his concern for contemporary relevance and his terminology are rightly understood, Tillich's idea of God can easily be reconciled with that of traditional Christian theism:

Tillich did not deny God or his distinction from created nature or from the thought of being. Rather he gave us an idea of God which conveys the necessary, intimate presence and involvement of God in cosmic events, human history and personal life, and which, at the same time, evokes a sense of awe and speechlessness by suggesting the ineffable mystery and majesty of God

. . . Far from having been an atheist, Tillich has offered us a weapon against atheism.[1]

Leslie Dewart, while rejecting both, asserts the basic identity of Tillich's final idea of God with the *Ipsum Esse* (Being Itself) of the scholastic tradition.[2]

But not everyone who is familiar with Tillich is ready to accept such easy harmonization. One of the best contemporary experts on the problem of God, D. Fabro, in his monumental history of atheism, entitles the chapter on Tillich: "Existential Reason Dissolved into Atheism."[3] G. Weigel's evaluation of Tillich is in the same vein:

> The first feeling of uneasiness a Catholic experiences on reading Tillich is that his supernaturalism (a term he does not like) is, on ultimate reduction, purest naturalism. He rejects natural theology on principle, but his whole theology is not only a natural theology, but more ominously a naturalistic theology. The final chapter of his *The Courage to Be* can have a depressing effect, for it seems to equate God with the basic energy at work in the universe, but interpreted in terms of human concern.[4]

In the pages that follow I will attempt to examine what makes such conflicting interpretations of Tillich possible. Thereby I hope to come closer to answering the initial question, i.e., whether or not, and if so, in what manner, Tillich prepared, unintentionally, the way for radical theology.

The starting point of Tillich is an existential one: the ultimate concern which awakens in man when he becomes aware of the danger that he may lose his life. Under the shock of experiencing "non-being," he discovers his own finitude. But in

[1]C. Kiesling, "A Translation of Tillich's Idea of God," *Journal of Ecumenical Studies,* Winter, 1967, pp. 714-715.

[2]See Leslie Dewart, *The Future of Belief: Theism in a World Come of Age* (New York: Herder & Herder, 1966), pp. 37-42.

[3]D. Fabro, *God in Exile* (Glen Rock, N. J.: Paulist/Newman. 1967).

[4]"The Theological Significance of Paul Tillich," *Paul Tillich in Catholic Thought,* ed. by Thomas A. O'Meara and Celestin D. Weisser (Dubuque, Iowa: The Priory Press), p. 17.

discovering his own finitude, man awakens to an implicit awareness of the Infinite; in experiencing his own conditional existence, he has an oblique but immediate knowledge (beyond and before any explicit rational knowledge) of the unconditional. This state of being ultimately concerned is faith for Tillich.

True faith does not only tolerate, but demands, an element of radical doubt for Tillich. To him this is the only logical extension of the Lutheran principle of justification by faith alone to the realm of knowledge. "Not only he who is in sin, but also he who is in doubt is justified through faith."[5] Therefore faith is a state, a state of ultimate concern, not faith in an object. If it were faith in an object (were this object God himself conceived as a Supreme Being), that would not justify the sinner; he would be justified by his own work, for, according to the Kantian epistemological presuppositions of Tillich, an object of the intellect is always a *creation* of the intellect.[6] Thus a faith which is primarily a faith *in* the God of theism, a distinct Supreme Being, is an idolatrous faith that is to be surpassed. If one's faith is genuine, he will deny any absolute certainty about any concrete content of faith.[7] Even if he despairs completely about the existence of God, about finding the truth at all, as long as he is seriously concerned in his "status of doubt" he is "in the status of faith." "And if all this comes together and you are desperate about the meaning of life, the seriousness of your despair is the expression of the meaning in which you still are living. This unconditional seriousness is the expression of the presence of the divine in the experience of utter separation from it."[8]

---

[5]Quoted from *The Protestant Era* published in part by Thomas J. J. Altizer in *Toward a New Christianity. Readings in the Death of God Theology* (New York: Harcourt, 1967), p. 162.
[6]See more on this in P. Tillich, *Systematic Theology* (Chicago: University of Chicago Press, 1967), I, 71-75.
[7]See *Dynamics of Faith* (New York: Harper & Row, 1956), p. 17.
[8]*The Protestant Era,* p. 162.

Tillich, of course, recognizes that man's ultimate concern must have a correlate; it must be a concern about *something.* Nevertheless, that which is man's ultimate concern lies beyond the object-subject scheme, since no mere object (something which is distinct from his being) can stir him up to be ultimately concerned. Man can be ultimately concerned only about that which can save or threaten his being. (Tillich understands by the being of man the whole human reality, the structure, meaning, and aim of one's existence.) Therefore, the object of ultimate concern must be both the ground of my being and infinitely surpassing, *transcending* my being. It is above and beyond me, yet I myself am rooted in it.[9] This correlate of man's ultimate concern is called "the ground of his being" or the "ground of being in general," "the power of being," or "being itself," all symbolic expressions for that which cannot be expressed: God. No statement other than the symbolic can be made about God.[10] A symbolic or a conceptual statement derived thereof, although it points toward God, is not only inadequately representative of the Infinite, but can not even be affirmed as unambiguously true. To do so would necessarily result in claiming ultimacy and absoluteness for a symbol which is created and therefore non-ultimate and relative. Thus the final consequence would be erecting idols. It follows, therefore, from the very nature of authentic faith that the believer simultaneously believes and doubts the concrete symbols and conceptual representations of his faith. The only criterion which decides whether or not his faith is genuine is a merely subjective one: it is the quality of his concern which becomes manifest in the radical seriousness of both his believing and his doubting.

Tillich is not only an existentialist, but, starting out with the

---

[9] See *Systematic Theology* I, 237-238.

[10] There is a certain development in Tillich on this point. In the first volume of his *Systematic Theology* he asserts that "God is being itself" is the only non-symbolic statement about God (see I, 238). Later in the same work, he modifies his position by claiming that every statement about God (including God as being itself) is necessarily symbolic (see II, 9).

analysis of the actual human existence, he builds up an impressive ontological system in the tradition of Heidegger, Hegel, and Schelling.[11] The existential analysis of the human situation has revealed that man is continuously threatened by destruction and non-being. This is so because man has distanced himself from the ground of his being; he is estranged from it. The present state of disruption and alienation, however, presupposes a primordial state of essential unity between man and his ground of being, i.e., an essential unity between man and God. This was a state before creation. Man did not yet exist, i.e., he did not "stand upon himself," did not actualize himself in freedom. Yet, in a sense, man "was," for he was "hidden" in the divine ground of life, "in an essential state beyond potentiality and actuality," "in the state of dreaming innocence," as it is mythologically described in the Paradise story of Genesis.[12]

The creation of man and the fall coincide in Tillich's system. Man is good insofar as the essential nature of man is good. But the creation of man is fulfilled through his free self-actualization. When man freely chooses to realize himself as a creature, he can only break away from his creative ground with which (or with whom) he has been one in the state of innocence.[13] The actualization of a creaturely existence and freedom is unavoidably connected with an estrangement from God. There is an abyss now between the essential state and the concrete existence of man. Man, as he exists now, is in a paradoxical condition; since he is separated from the infinite ground of being, he is constantly exposed to annihilation. Nevertheless, he is not totally cut off from the ground of being, or else he would cease to exist.

He "remembers" the primordial condition of unity, and there-

---

[11]The tradition, of course, should be traced back to Platonism and gnosticism, to which the German idealism is heavily indebted.

[12]*Systematic Theology,* I, 259.

[13]*Ibid.,* p. 256; II, 44-47.

fore he can ask the question of God. Traditional natural theology is valid insofar as it restricts itself to formulating this
question as a result of reflecting on man's experience of finitude.
But as soon as natural theology, forgetting about the state
of estrangement of the human reason, claims to know God, it
creates an idol, a "Supreme Being who is nothing but the prolongation of the finite categories of man's world." Any knowledge of God which answers man's question implied in the philosophical analysis of Being can be received by man only as a
revelation from God himself.[14]

Thus the relationship of "existential man" (man in the state
of estrangement) to God can be summed up by the symbolic
statement: God is man's ground of being from which (or from
whom) man is estranged. Tillich has chosen the word *ground*,
for, in its symbolic use, it points beyond the finite categories of
cause and substance. God is neither a caused cause, nor a substance which is entirely expressed in its accidents. As first cause,
it underlies the entire series of causes and effects; and as ultimate substance, it underlies the whole process of becoming;
yet it is an underlying in which substance (God) and accidents (creatures) preserve their mutual freedom. Moreover,
in Tillich's mind, to be created free generates necessarily an
opposition between the freedom of God and that of his creature. The creature feels guilty about it, since by freely actualiz-
ing himself, he is freely estranged from God, yet at the same
time, this free estrangement is his unavoidable destiny.[15]

On the one hand, as far as creation in general is concerned,
Tillich maintains that creation is not a necessary act of God,
since God does not depend on anything which is beyond or
above him. He is freely related to his creatures.[16] On the other
hand, Tillich implies that God could not have abstained from
creating, since "divine life and divine creativity are not dif-

---

[14]*Ibid.*, I, 64-70.
[15]*Ibid.*, I, 238.
[16]*Ibid.*, I, 252; II, 5-8.

ferent." "Creation is not only God's freedom but also his destiny."[17] God goes out of himself in creation, participates in the history of the world, so that everything that happens in the universe has an "eternal dimension" which is "the Divine Life itself." In a sense, God is complemented by his creation, since "the eternal act of creation is driven by a love which finds fulfillment only through the other one who has the freedom to reject and to accept love."[18]

There has been only one man in human history in which essential manhood, i.e., the primordial unity of God and man, has appeared under the conditions of existence without being conquered by its tragic vicissitudes; this man was Jesus as the Christ. In spite of his participation in the ambiguities of human life, he maintained an "unbreakable unity of his being with that of the ground of all being. . . . In all his utterances, words, deeds, and sufferings, he is transparent to that which he represents as the Christ, the divine mystery . . . The acceptance of the cross, both during his life and at the end of it, is the decisive test of his unity with God." On the cross, he totally sacrifices himself "as a historical individual"; he negates everything that is merely finite and human in him, so that he may become fully transparent "to that in him which is greater than he." Thus Jesus who sacrificed himself as Jesus, to himself as the Christ, has become the only adequate symbol of God, because he expresses not only the ultimate, but also his own lack of ultimacy.[19] This is the sense in which Tillich accepts the two traditional titles of Christ and equates their meaning. Christ is both Son of Man and Son of God. He is Son of Man insofar as he is the essential man, and Son of God insofar as essential manhood present in human existence means precisely the total unity of man with, and his utter transparency to, the ground of his being, God.

[17]*Ibid.*, I, 252.
[18]*Ibid.*, III, 422.
[19]*Ibid.*, I, 135.

Jesus as the Christ has become the carrier of the "New Being"; he is the one in whom estranged mankind will be reunited to its divine ground.[20] Tillich does not deny the existential uncertainty of individual salvation; in virtue of his system, however, he is inclined to assume that, eventually, the whole of creation returns to union with God.[21] He rejects eternal condemnation "as a contradiction in terms." In Tillich's ontology, it would really be an absurdity, since it would imply that the "demonic" (the estrangement which is the split in being) would reach the very heart of being, i.e., it would somehow affect God himself.[22] Eternal death, a "self-exclusion from eternal life and consequently from being," is also denied, though after some hesitation. Such a doctrine would "contradict the idea of God's permanent creation of the finite as something 'very good' . . . nothing that is can become completely evil. If something is, if it has being, it is included in the creative divine love."[23]

Moreover, although Tillich insists that every individual person is unique and will participate as a conscious individual self in Eternal Life, yet "essentialization," i.e., the reunion of estranged mankind with the ground of being is a "matter of universal participation." If only one man were eternally condemned, all were condemned, since, in the essence of one individual, the essences of all beings are present. Vice versa, those individuals who are in a more advanced stage toward reaching their essential being will help "by participation" those who are still in the despair of total self-rejection.

Such a short resumé of Tillich's system cannot do justice to his complex and highly nuanced thought. In fact, the whole system becomes multivalent by his repeated warnings that every positive statement needs to be complemented by its very negation. Tillich does not mean this in the sense of the traditional triple way of affirmation, negation, and supereminence. As has

---

[20]*Ibid.*, II, 168-169.
[21]*Ibid.*, III, 416-418.
[22]*Ibid.*, I, 285.
[23]*Ibid.*, III, 407-408.

been seen, he frequently affirms and denies simultaneously the same thing under the same aspect. Therefore, it is relatively easy to isolate a series of statements which can convincingly show that Tillich is both orthodox and highly successful in presenting the Christian message in a new and relevant language to modern man. And undoubtedly, this is his avowed and sincere intention. But it is equally easy to point out other aspects in his thought which show that there is a basic monistic undercurrent in his interpretation of "being." Altizer and Hamilton do not proceed arbitrarily when they classify Tillich as one of those theologians who prepared their theology.[24] In what follows I will attempt to summarize those features of Tillich's thought which point toward the death-of-God theology.

Man before creation is not simply an idea of God; he *is* in his essential state. Therein he is united to God, not by a free initiative of God's grace (grace qualifies only the subsequent creative and saving activity of God), but "essentially." The oneness with God is of man's inmost nature and is so perfect as to establish an identity. This is suggested by the fact that Tillich describes the subsequent existence of man as an estrangement from himself, an estrangement from his ground of being, and an estrangement from God, whereby "himself," "ground of being," and "God" are used as interchangeable and synonymous terms.

That the primordial union of man and God has been conceived in a pantheistic way is further confirmed by Tillich's assertion that the revelation of the mystery of God has become necessary only because man's reason has been estranged from its own divine depth. It is only the dialectic of existential estrangement introducing the "undecided and unfinished manifoldedness of the real" against the "structural oneness of everything within the Absolute" that tends to balance the pantheistic element in Tillich's system.[25] But as G. McLean concludes, "the

---

[24]See *Radical Theology and the Death of God*, pp. 199-200.
[25]*Systematic Theology*, I, 235.

pantheistic element . . . is balanced only by his dialectic and not eliminated."[26]

Tillich insists that the Incarnation can mean only the appearance of essential manhood in Jesus the Christ. Essential manhood, however, means essential God-manhood, the eternal unity of God and man. Notice again that the essential God-manhood which has become manifest in Christ is the original "natural" state of man, not the result of a qualitatively unique grace-act granted only to one man (which could be an acceptable Christian interpretation). The ambiguity of his christology can be summed up in this formula: since Jesus the Christ is the ideal man, he is the eternal God-man who appeared in human history. This reveals most sharply the pantheistic thrust of Tillich's thought: the distinctive line between God and man is only the intermediate phase of a dialectic process: in the beginning there is no distinction; at the eschatological end, when all mankind will participate in the New Being of Christ, the distinction becomes dimmed again. The history of the universe and of man in particular, with all its tragic vicissitudes and its final "elevation of everything positive into Eternal Life," can be interpreted as the history of "Being Itself" who is the "God above God" of Tillich.

As has been seen, J. A. T. Robinson takes over from Tillich the symbol of God as "the self-transcendent ground of Being" in all its ambiguity and makes it the foundation of his doctrine of God. Not being familiar with the ontological system of Tillich (the only work he quotes is the sermon collection *The Shaking of the Foundations*) within which alone his doctrine of God can be properly understood, he mixes without any scruples the Tillichian doctrine of God with the rather different and even contrasting ideas of Bonhoeffer, Bultmann, and Buber.[27]

---

[26]G. F. McLean, "Symbol and Analogy: Tillich and Thomas," in O'Meara and Weisser, eds., *op. cit.*, p. 178.

[27]E.g., Robinson does not notice that Bonhoeffer rejects metaphysics as resulting in religion which has to go, while Tillich builds a new metaphysics and attempts to uncover the religious depth dimension of the whole of reality.

Evidently, Altizer and Hamilton do not fully agree with Tillich. Evaluating his work as a significant contribution which paved the way for radical theology, they accuse him of having stopped at a half-way point. For them, "the ground of being" is not radically immanent enough. They hail his rejection of the God of theism, a God who is a distinct Supreme Being. But they are dissatisfied with Tillich's insistence that God is the *transcendent* depth dimension of all reality. In their eyes, the mistake of Tillich is that he did not entirely collapse transcendence into immanence.[28]

In his anthology, *Toward a New Christianity: Readings in the Death of God Theology* (p. 155), Altizer publishes an excerpt from *The Protestant Era* of Tillich with satisfaction and approval, as "one of his [Tillich's] most lucid and revealing writings." He is obviously pleased with the Tillichian thesis that authentic faith *must* include an element of radical doubt. This, in Altizer's interpretation, means that contemporary faith in a transcendent God is possible only in the form of radical doubt. So Tillich, against his own intention, confirms the thesis of Altizer: in our age, faith as a firm intellectual assent to belief in a transcendent God is impossible. And, since in Altizer's mind God does not exist independently from human consciousness, the death of faith in God means the death of God himself.

Although Altizer does not mention it, his dialectic system is remarkably similar to that of Tillich. Both consider creation as an unavoidable fall from a state of natural oneness with God, which leads through a stage of estrangement to an apocalyptic reunion of the human and the divine. For both, it is Christ in whom the estrangement is universally overcome. For Altizer, this cosmic process is unambiguously the dialectic development of God himself, who, dying to his transcendent form in Christ,

---

[28]See especially W. Hamilton, "America and the Future of Theology," *Radical Theology and the Death of God*, p. 11; also *Toward a New Christianity: Readings in the Death of God Theology*, pp. 7-9.

conquers the abyss of estrangement between himself and his creation. He becomes his precise opposite: the completely secular world, in order to bring about a final synthesis where all tension between transcendent and immanent, divine and human, is eliminated forever. The final product of the process is rather Man taking the place of God than God re-uniting his creature with himself. In Tillich, too, the cosmic process can be called the history of God, or, using the Tillichian name for God, the history of Being Itself. Yet, Tillich inserts into his system many balancing counterpoints which make it more Christian and traditional. These built-in checks and balances, however, do not eliminate the possibility of a monistic interpretation. But in Tillich's theology it is not Man who absorbs God, but rather God, transcending any particular being, yet inseparably bound to all of them, who "fulfills himself" in Man.

7

KARL BARTH

Barth is the most passionate defender of God's "wholly otherness." He advocates "the infinite qualitative difference" of Kierkegaard, the unfathomable chasm between God and man, with more vehemence than either Bultmann or Tillich. Yet, paradoxically, Altizer, van Buren, and Hamilton depend more closely on Barth than on Bultmann or Tillich. They acknowledge that they are indebted to him more than to any other theologian of the twentieth century (with the exception of Bonhoeffer). Rather than try to sum up the complex and developing thought of Barth, a task which has been successfully accomplished both by Catholic and Protestant theologians in the past, I will concentrate on throwing into relief those points of his docrine which, unintentionally, prepared the way for the conclusions of the death-of-God theologians.[1]

The early Barth believed that his duty was to fight on a double front: liberal Protestantism and Catholicism. According to him, liberal Protestantism had lost the very substance of faith; faith had been reduced to the highest possibility of *human* reason, revelation to the highest peak of *human* history, the God-consciousness of Jesus to the highest realization of *human* religiosity. In his judgment, the ultimate result of this reduction-

---

[1] In outlining the thought of Barth and in analyzing his *The Epistle to the Romans,* I heavily draw upon the work of H. Urs von Balthasar, *Karl Barth: Darstellung und Deutung seiner Theologie* (Köln: Hegner) which, in the judgment of Barth himself, is a faithful and penetrating exposition of his theology.

ism was represented most clearly in the philosophy of Feuerbach, who identified Christianity with a doctrine about man, and in the movement of the "German Christians," who openly aligned themselves with the neo-paganism of the Nazi regime.

Barth was equally opposed to Catholicism. He admitted, however, that, while liberal Protestantism had thrown overboard all of Christianity but the name, Catholicism had saved the Christian substance, but in a distorted form. Catholic theology had both preserved and relativized revelation. The relationship between God and man was determined by a philosophical "pre-knowledge" (*Vorverständnis*) which is natural theology based on the doctrine of the analogy of being. Therefore, the place of Christ is *a priori* defined by an ontological system which is conceived prior to revelation and cannot "be torn apart" by it. Thus, the revelation of Christ is deprived of its absolute claim. It only fulfills and surpasses the natural order, and, in particular, a natural philosophical knowledge of God, but it is not the foundation of *all* true knowledge of God. In the final analysis, Catholicism commits the same sin as liberal Protestantism: man attempts to rule over God, to grasp dominion over him. By emphasizing both nature *and* grace, intellect *and* revelation, faith *and* free human cooperation, Catholicism makes God depend on man; it is as much a sinful assault against God ("Bemächtigung Gottes, Griff nach Gott") as that of liberal Protestantism.[2]

The main concern of the early Barth can be understood only in this context: he cannot stress enough the infinite distance, the *diakrisis*, between God and man. He wants to ban all disrespectful attempts of man to take God's place or to abase God to man's level. The passionate zeal for safeguarding God's sovereignty and total otherness is the basic motive which underlies and explains the whole of Barth's thought. The later Barth, however, became more and more aware that the transcendence of God does not exclude his presence to his creation;

[2]Cf. von Balthasar, *op. cit.,* p. 54.

on the contrary, it is precisely God's infinite qualitative otherness which enables him to be intimately present to each of his
creatures, without jeopardizing the autonomy of the creature or
his own divinity. But it is not the mature Barth who influenced
radical theology. Altizer and Hamilton reject the theology of
Church Dogmatics or *The Humanity of God* as too traditional
and orthodox. But the impact of the early Barth, in particular,
the disturbing message of his commentary on *The Epistle to the
Romans* (second revised edition in 1921), decisively shaped the
thought of Altizer and Hamilton.[a] We are witnessing here a
strange unintentional dialectic process: the one-sided insistence on God's transcendence as total otherness has unavoidably led, implicitly in the early Barth, explicitly in radical
theology, to its opposite extreme: the identification of God
and man.

Analyzing primarily the second edition of *The Epistle to the
Romans*, I intend to investigate why and how this dialectic
shift has taken place. In *The Epistle to the Romans,* God and
man stand against each other as pure mutual contradiction:
God is the pure negation of man, and man, precisely as man,
is the pure negation of God; God is being, man is nothingness; God is holiness, and man, in his very essence, is sinfulness.
The most fundamental drive of man is *eros*, concupiscence, a
selfish, sinful demonic instinct. God is therefore the enemy of
man; man is under the condemning judgment, the *krisis* of
God.

This absolute opposition excludes any possibility on the part of
man to know God. Every type of natural theology is nothing but a
sacrilegious attempt by man to surpass his limits; he wants to
know God by infinitely intensifying all human perfections and
by applying them to a Supreme Being. The end result is necessarily a man-made projection, an idol which Feuerbach's cri-

---

[a]See, e.g., *Toward a New Christianity: Readings in the Death of God
Theology,* pp. 1-13; 123-140. Van Buren's thought has been shaped, not
only by the early Barth, but also by the christocentrism of Barth's *Church
Dogmatics*.

tique has rightly destroyed once and for all. God is not in continuity with human perfections; his perfections are totally other than what we can conceive. The only way in which God can be known in this world by sinful man is to discover and affirm the absolute distance between God and the world, to see nothing in the world but the eclipse, the absence of God. Religious culture and religious philosophies obscure this fundamental strangeness of God in the world. Barth, therefore, looks with a certain appreciation upon atheism and a purely secular culture which does not attempt to create idols, but affirms honestly the absence of anything divine in the world.

The absolute contradictory opposition, proclaimed and insisted upon with such passionate fervor, conceals, nevertheless, a hidden identity. Barth protests unceasingly against "the divinization of man and the humanization of God in the form of a romantic immediacy." He denounces its traces in the first edition of *The Epistle to the Romans*. But in spite of his efforts to eliminate every remnant of a gnostic Hegelian dialectic from his theology, the Hegelian substructure still survives, even in the second revised edition of *The Epistle to the Romans*. This sort of affirmation is evident in several sections of the commentary:

> Originally, there was no separation. Men dwelt in the Garden of Eden, in which there were no absolute and relative, no 'higher' and 'lower', no 'there' and 'here': such distinctions marked the Fall. The world was originally one with the Creator, and men were one with God. The natural order, then, as such, was holy, because holiness is its characteristic mark.[4]

But this pure and peaceful existence in which God and man "were one and not two" has been irretrievably sundered;[5] the fall of man coincided with his creation: he fell out of the im-

---

[4]Karl Barth, *The Epistle to the Romans,* transl. by E. C. Hoskyns (London, New York, Toronto: Oxford University Press, 1953), p. 247.
[5]*Ibid.,* p. 250.

mediate oneness with God when he became an autonomous self, became aware of himself as merely a man, a creature. "Men ought not to know that they are merely men."[6] It follows from this that religion is the fulcrum of sin because in religion man sets himself in relationship to God. But to do so means to affirm himself as a distinct self from God. And this is rebellion against God, the essence and root of all sins. Thus, paradoxically, when in the moment of being created, Eve rises to worship her Creator, she commits the first sin: "inasmuch as SHE worshipped HIM, she was separated from Him in a manner at once terrible and presumptuous."[7]

Yet God's judgment, in which the whole world is pronounced guilty and worthy of damnation, is simultaneously an act of salvation for the same world: God's absolute no goes over to absolute yes. All mankind has been declared guilty, but all mankind will be saved; i.e., it will return in the grace of Jesus Christ to original unity with God. The individual as such has no decisive role to play in this universal predestination to salvation. The original oneness with God, Creation-Fall, judgment, and return in Christ to the original unity with God are phases of a necessary dialectic process.

As the new "unobservable existential ego" of redeemed man is not his veritable ego, but the Holy Spirit himself, so his knowledge of God, which is faith, is in him, but is not really *his* knowledge. Faith is an act of God in man, but in no way can it be called an act of man. Only God can know God. The maximum man can do is to become an "empty room" (*Hohlraum*), a "bombshell crater" (*Einschlagstrichter*) into which God's word falls.[8]

This outline does not do justice to the intention and the whole message of *The Epistle to the Romans*. Undoubtedly, Barth intends to proclaim the Christian message, and nothing

---

[6]*Ibid.*, p. 247.
[7]*Ibid.*, pp. 247-248.
[8]*Ibid.*, pp. 35-42; 102-103; 296-297.

but the Christian message, as forcefully as possible. He certainly succeeded in this to a great extent. Yet, however passionately he protests against any philosophical speculation which dims the infinite distance between God and creature, the early Barth himself lacks a clearly defined concept of created being. Before creation and in the eschatological state, man is defined as immediately one with God; the very person of redeemed man coincides with the Holy Spirit. In the intermediate stage, between original unity and reunion, man as mere man *is* sheer nothingness, a sinful contradiction of God. Therefore, ultimately only God exists for Barth. The creature as creature is only a provisional phase in the dialectic process to return into the original unity out of which it has fallen. We may call this vision—to use a term of H. Urs von Balthasar—theopanism (God is everything), and this is a particular form of pantheism: an implicit but real identification of God and the world. Thus one cannot avoid the conclusion that in spite of (or perhaps because of) Barth's uncritical attacks on all religious philosophy, he inadvertently retains elements of a gnostic vision which fecundated German idealism, and, as has been seen, has influenced the thought of Tillich in many essential points. From these references to the philosophical presuppositions of *The Epistle to the Romans*, one can already surmise its impact on radical theology.

Altizer's original experience of the sacred is congenial to that of the early Barth. The reality of God and the reality of this world are contradictorily opposed: if one affirms the reality of this world, he can know God only as nothingness, as a complete void; but conversely, from the viewpoint of faith, the reality of God is so terribly real that "it dissolves all other reality whatsoever." Also for Altizer, as well as for Barth, Creation is identical with Fall. To exist as a creature *is* to be guilty, both for the early Barth and for the early Altizer. In Altizer's view, creation is a primal movement away from the original union with the divine. To be a distinct self means necessarily to be selfish, to be separated from the divine. Authentic Christianity is therefore the ultimate form of rebellion against man's own self; it cannot triumph unless man as a distinct self is ontologically destroyed. Genuine Christianity is "the absolute form of self-negation."[9] All this shows that the early Altizer expresses the Barthian contradiction in a much cruder form than Barth himself. The sacred and the profane, the kingdom of God and this world, God and the human self, are so *irreconcilably* opposed that one is the annihilation of the other.

Like Barth, Altizer cannot endure this absolute static opposition; in his later works he moves from the static to a dynamic dialectic which eventually resolves the tension. But unlike Barth, who remains on the side of the Transcendent Wholly Other, Altizer takes the other side; he has such dionysian hunger for a biological fullness of life, for energy, joy, love, flesh, in a word, for all that is secular, that after a first desperate effort he can no longer deny the reality of this world. But then, as a consequence, in virtue of his primal experience, he has to negate the reality of the transcendent God. God's lordship is no longer a reality, but a nightmare, a diabolic temptation. While for Barth the primal and final stage of the dialectic process is the transcendent God, for Altizer the transcendent God changes into its own opposite, the profane world, and the end result will be God fully and without remainder absorbed into man. In spite of this final divergence, however, it is the Barthian idea of divine transcendence (strengthened by Altizer's enthusiasm for Oriental mysticism) which forces Altizer to adopt his stand: in order to be able to affirm the full value and reality of man and of this world, he feels compelled to affirm the death of God.

W. Hamilton seems to have only a loose connection with Barthian theology: his early theological outlook was shaped by the neoorthodox movement in general. His idea of God was partially a watered-down version of the Barthian "enemy-

---

[9]Altizer, *Oriental Mysticism and Biblical Eschatology,* p. 193.

God" who is "present to man as terror or threat." The later "radical" Hamilton reacts to his earlier belief with resentment and disillusion. He can no longer hold on "by the finger-nails to the cliff of faith."[10] He no longer feels a horror of and a fear before God. Ready to accept the neo-orthodox critique of religion that man cannot know God, he is unable to accept the positive thesis: God makes himself known by his revealing Word. In the new secular mood which characterizes Hamilton's theology, the experience of the otherness of God is transformed into the experience of remoteness, absence, and irrelevance. He sometimes expresses hope that God will eventually "return," but he certainly does not expect the return of the Barthian "enemy God." He feels, as does Altizer, that this God is a mortal danger for the full value and autonomy of the secular world which the radical Christian has discovered with such enthusiasm. So Hamilton, too, is influenced by the Barthian idea of transcendence conceived as negation of this world to pronounce his "thesis": God is dead.

Van Buren also asserts Barth's influence in his attempt to reduce Christianity to a way of life centering around the man Jesus in whose contagious freedom the Christian shares. When opting for a non-cognitive approach to theological language, the decisive reason he gives is Barth's theological critique of natural theology.[11]

One cannot deny the logic of van Buren's position. If one admits that man as man by his own intellect has no ability whatsoever to discern the divine, then even if God himself speaks his word to man in Jesus Christ, man will not be able to know God, but only the man Jesus. In other words, the word *God* can mean for us exclusively and only the man Jesus of Nazareth.[12]

---

[10]W. Hamilton, "The Death of God Theologies Today," in *Radical Theology and the Death of God*, p. 35.
[11]See van Buren, *The Secular Meaning of the Gospel*, p. 98.
[12]*Ibid.*, pp. 146-147.

8

DIETRICH BONHOEFFER

Besides Barth, another major influence on radical theology is undoubtedly Dietrich Bonhoeffer. But while it was the early Barth who shaped the thinking of the radical theologians, in Bonhoeffer's case only his last two posthumously published works, *Ethics*[1] and *Letters and Papers from Prison,*[2] or more precisely, some fragments of these two works, inspired Robinson, Hamilton and van Buren.[3] The scope of my study will be restricted to investigating this last phase of Bonhoeffer's theological development as it appears in the posthumous fragments, especially in his last letters, those written between April, 1944, and his execution by the Nazis in May, 1945. The analysis of these fragments (evidently to be made in the context of the whole of Bonhoeffer's personal and theological development) will shed light, I hope, on one of the most ironic facts of theological history: a man about whom one of his prison-mates testified after the war that "he was one of the very few men . . . that I have ever met to whom his God was real and close to him" has become a decisive factor in shaping a theology without God.[4]

With the prison letter of April 30, 1944, a new phase

---

[1] Dietrich Bonhoeffer, *Ethics* (New York: Macmillan, 1965).

[2] Dietrich Bonhoeffer, *Letters and Papers from Prison* (New York: Macmillan, 1962).

[3] In fact, Bonhoeffer's influence is not limited to this small group, but embraces more and more the whole of the American theological scene, both Protestant and Catholic. See H. Cox, "Beyond Bonhoeffer?" *Commonweal,* September 17, 1965, pp. 653-657.

[4] *Letters,* pp. 13-14.

emerges in the life and thinking of Bonhoeffer. I would like to stress that *both* his life and his thinking entered a new stage. In Bonhoeffer's career, theology and life, reflection and existential commitment always developed in close interaction. The new phase cannot be written off, as some theologians have suggested, as the agony of an unbalanced and confused mind exhausted by the long sustained sufferings of imprisonment. On the contrary, everything seems to indicate that, after a period of tension, anguish, and inability to work, Bonhoeffer again mastered his situation:

> For a long time I haven't been able to get down to any serious work, but with the approach of spring I'm feeling more in the mood for it again.[5]

He is fascinated by his new intuitions. He believes that these mark a new beginning, not just for his own thinking, but for theology in general. Neither the more and more frequent air-raids, nor the growing certainty about his inevitable fate disturb his work. After the alarm is over, he immediately returns to writing his notes. Not even the failure of the attempted coup against Hitler's life shakes his serenity and peace.[6]

While it would be unjust to discard the last letters as not truly an integral part of Bonhoeffer's theological development, it would be equally unwarranted and would run against the very intention of Bonhoeffer himself to take these notes as a mature and well-rounded expression of his new insights. Much of what he wrote in the last months of his life has been lost, and what remains are private letters addressed to his friend, E. Bethge. Bonhoeffer was well aware that his ideas were not mature enough to be published in book form. He dared only to confide them to his best friend and permitted Bethge only reluctantly, at his own discretion, to send these letters to some

---

[5] *Ibid.*, p. 160.
[6] *Ibid.*, pp. 162, 225-227.

common friends. Bonhoeffer insisted that he was writing only to clarify his own mind and apologized to Bethge for "putting it all so clumsily and badly."[7]

Therefore, anyone who would interpret correctly the last fragments of Bonhoeffer will have to avoid two extremes: belittling their importance as if they did not represent the mind of the "real Bonhoeffer," or taking them as the definitive expression of a new synthesis. They have to be valued for what they are: a first groping attempt to express a new vision which was prepared by his whole life and theology. Yet once expressed, the radicality of this vision surprised even Bonhoeffer himself.

His new insights center around two major themes: the problem of "the world come of age" and "the non-religious interpretation of Christianity." But these ideas will necessarily be misunderstood unless one sees them as attempts to answer a more basic question which is the main concern of Bonhoeffer: "The thing that keeps coming back to me is. . . . who is Christ for us today?"[8] In fact, this question sums up the quest of Bonhoeffer's whole life. Beginning with his first work, *Sanctorum Communio,*[9] up to his last letters, his faith in the crucified and risen Christ remained firm and unshaken. He knew with the certitude of a peacefully possessed personal faith that Christ has been, is, and will be the Lord and center of the world. He was also convinced from the very beginning that the transcendence of God means, not His distance from us, but His free gift of Himself to us. He "is not free of man but free for man."[10] Christ is the Word of His freedom to man. The very structure of the being of Christ is to be for me, to be contemporaneous with me, to be "haveable" by me.[11] Christ is present for me

[7]*Ibid.,* p. 224.

[8]*Ibid.,* p. 162.

[9]American edition: *Communion of Saints* (New York: Harper & Row, 1961).

[10]Dietrich Bonhoeffer, *Act and Being* (New York: Harper & Row, 1966).

[11]See Dietrich Bonhoeffer, *Christ the Center* (New York: Harper & Row, 1966).

here and now in the concrete sociological reality: the community of the Church. More precisely, the humiliated and risen Christ exists *as* the Church. The one who is chosen as a disciple hears His call in the Scriptures of the Church, becomes free from the world, and is conformed to Christ through the sacraments and in the fellowship of the Church.[12] Yet the more the disciple recognizes the *exclusive* Lordship of Christ, the more its *universal* character becomes evident.

There is an inner logic and clear direction in the development of Bonhoeffer's thought from *The Cost of Discipleship* and *Life Together* to the bold vision of *Ethics* and his last letters from prison. Becoming *free from the world* in order to be conformed to Christ in the fellowship of the Church is not an escape from the world into the shelter of an exclusive salvation club. On the contrary, conformity to, and participation in, the existence of Christ means *to be free,* as he was, *for the world.* Therefore, on the one hand, Bonhoeffer's return from abroad to Nazi-dominated Germany, his conscious acceptance of sharing the tragic destiny of his nation, and finally his participation in the resistance movement against Nazism were the concrete realization of his christological principle: to be a Christian means participation in the existence of Christ who lived, suffered, and died for the world. On the other hand, his increasing contacts with many honest and responsible unbelievers in the conspiracy led him to ask the question of his life again in a more universalistic perspective than before: "Who is Christ for us today?" and here "for us" includes all mankind living today whose majority consists of unbelievers. Or in more explicit terms: "How can Christ become the Lord even of those with no religion?"[13] Let me insist again that Bonhoeffer is deeply convinced that Christ is "in deed and in truth the Lord

---

[12]See Dietrich Bonhoeffer, *The Cost of Discipleship* (New York: Macmillan, 1963), as well as his *Life Together* (New York: Harper, 1954).
    [13]*Letters,* pp. 162-163.

of the world" even of the unbelievers.[14] His problem is the meaning of this Lordship for contemporary man, especially for those who are not religiously inclined. This christological background has been neglected by many interpreters, although it is a necessary prerequisite for grasping what Bonhoeffer really meant by the terms *world come of age* and *non-religious interpretation of Christianity*. Both concepts are inseparably tied up with his christology.

There is development and even a real change of position in Bonhoeffer's thought concerning the value of man and of the world. The earliest part of *Ethics* sees the autonomy of man, his knowledge of good and evil, his ability to choose between them and to judge the ethical quality of his choice as a manifestation of man's basic sinfulness.[15] Like Barth, at this stage Bonhoeffer also affirms that man insofar as he is a distinct self and knows himself as a distinct self "besides God" and "outside of God" is sinful. All this is the result of the original fall by which man has lost his primordial simple unity with God. In this theological framework no distinction is possible between a sinful attempt of man to absolute autonomy by taking the place of God, and a relative but real autonomy of man made free and responsible by God the Creator. Bonhoeffer cannot as yet see any positive value in the responsible freedom of man which enables him to choose freely what Catholic theology calls "natural good." Bonhoeffer's only concern at this stage is to show how Christ restores the original unity of God and man.

In a later' chapter of the *Ethics* Bonhoeffer approaches again the problem of autonomy, but evaluates it now in a more positive sense.[16] Although man's autonomy is still regarded as the

---

[14]*Ibid.*, p. 164. My christological interpretation of the key concepts of the *Letters* is based on E. Bethge, *Dietrich Bonhoeffer: Eine Biographie* (Munich: Kaiser, 1967), pp. 958-1000: "Die Neue Theologie, ein Exkurs"; and J. Moltmann and J. Weissbach, *Two Studies in the Theology of Bonhoeffer* (New York: Scribner's, 1967).

[15]See *Ethics*, pp. 17-54.

[16]See "The Last Things and Things Before the Last," *Ethics*, pp. 120-187.

result of the fall, Bonhoeffer now distinguishes a good use and an abuse of human freedom. He recognizes a place in Christianity for natural and this-worldly values (primarily in the realm of ethics). Whatever is good, honest, decent, and human cannot be irrelevant from the viewpoint of the Christian. He calls all these merely but truly human values "the penultimate" (*das Vorletzte*). On the other hand, the penultimate is not a final value in itself. Its worth and meaning derive from its orientation to what is final: the consummation of the redemption of the universe by Christ. On the other hand, although the penultimate cannot deserve or force the final coming of Christ, in some way it still prepares his coming. The radical Barthians are mistaken in claiming that God's redeeming word is an absolute destruction of our world. It is destruction, but also preservation and transformation of whatever is valuable in our world. Neither pole, neither the penultimate nor the ultimate, should be absolutized and set in an absolute opposition against the other. This would serve to separate God the Creator from God the Redeemer and would sever the unity of Jesus Christ, the God-man who unites the reality of God and man in one. Since Jesus Christ is man, we also may be and must be men before God. Since God has laid bare and condemned the sinfulness of man and of the world on the cross of Christ, the Christian also has to condemn the sinfulness of the penultimate (man and his world). But the Christian also affirms and embraces this world with optimism and enthusiasm, since the risen Christ has reconciled the world to God and he is the pledge of the world's final eschatological renewal. So the "worldliness" of Bonhoeffer, his esteem of human values, can be understood only in the context of his christology: the oneness of the Creator and the Redeemer God, the Incarnation, Crucifixion, and Resurrection of Christ.

Bonhoeffer, however, is not satisfied with merely stating these truths. The Church, and the Christian in the Church, not only believe, but truly share in the work of Christ. The

Church takes upon herself the guilt of the world, acknowledging it as her own guilt. Thus by participating in the sufferings of Christ, she becomes the place of forgiveness and renewal for the world.

Letters and Papers from Prison constitutes a new step forward in shaping a theology of the world. In this last phase of his life and work, the two correlative motives of the *Ethics* reach a crescendo. The more painfully he shares in the sufferings of God for the world, the more firmly and wholeheartedly he embraces everything which is good for the world:

> Our joy is hidden in suffering, our life in death. But all through we are sustained in a wondrous fellowship. To all this God in Jesus has given his Yea and his Amen, and that is the firm ground on which we stand. In these turbulent times we are always forgetting what it is that makes life really worthwhile . . . if this earth was good enough for the man Jesus Christ, if a man like him really lived in it, then, and only then, has life a meaning for us. If Jesus had not lived, then our life, in spite of all the other people we know and honour and love, would be without meaning . . . The word "meaning" does occur in the Bible, but it is only a translation of what the Bible means by "promise."[17]

His affirmation of the world, his optimism expands even under the growing shadow of his imminent execution. It grows because it is based on his increasing participation in the life-giving cross of Christ:

> This is what I mean by worldliness—taking life in one's stride, with all its duties and problems, its successes and failures, its experiences and helplessness. It is in such a life that we throw ourselves utterly in the arms of God and participate in his sufferings in the world and watch with Christ in Gethsemane. That is faith, that is *metanoia,* and that is what makes a man and a Christian . . . How can success make us arrogant or failure lead

---

[17]*Letters*, pp. 243-244.

us astray, when we participate in the sufferings of God by living in this world?[18]

The growing appreciation of the world in its relative autonomy based on the creating, preserving, and redeeming action of Christ helps Bonhoeffer evaluate positively the historical process of secularization by which the world has "come of age." This means for him that man, particularly by his human reason, has emancipated himself from any kind of tutelage. He no longer needs God as a "stop-gap," as an ultimate hypothesis in morals, in politics, in science, or in philosophy. Man has demonstrated that every problem, moral, political, scientific, or philosophical, can be solved without any recourse to God. Religion is, therefore, continuously in retreat. It still claims certain unenlightened corners of human knowledge and existence where there is still "place for God," like "the inner life of the soul," or the limit-problems of anxiety, suffering, and death. But what will happen if, one day, man will be able to solve all these problems without the help of a God-hypothesis?[19]

Bonhoeffer is not disturbed by the phenomenon of man's coming of age and by God's subsequent "retreat." He clearly recognizes the dangers in man's growing autonomy; it may lead to man's claim of absolute freedom, to his self-deification, which would necessarily result in man's slavery and dehumanization.[20] But his hope prevails over his anxiety about the future of man. He expects that the process of secularization will become "a clearing of the decks for the God of the Bible."[21] The God of religion, namely, the God used as a "stop-gap" scientific hypothesis, or even the God of philosophy, is nothing else in Bonhoeffer's view but a prolongation of our world, man's own creation and, therefore, in the ultimate analysis, a false idol. This is why the gradual retreat of this "God" fills Bon-

[18]*Ibid.*, pp. 226-227.
[19]*Ibid.*, pp. 194-196; 211-220.
[20]*Ibid.*, p. 237. More in detail, *Ethics*, pp. 88-119.
[21]*Letters*, p. 220.

hoeffer with thrilling expectation and joy.

Thus the analysis of Bonhoeffer's idea of the "world come of age" has led us to consider the other fundamental notion of his latest writings: the Christian God as opposed to the God of religion, in other words, the task of a "non-religious interpretation of Christianity."

Besides the "non-religious interpretation of Christianity," Bonhoeffer uses a wide range of similar terms which all point in the same direction, but reveal the complexity of the underlying experience that Bonhoeffer tries to communicate to his friend: "worldly interpretation," "the new non-religious language," "religionless Christianity," "to be a Christian without religion," "to live without religion." Already a simple review of the terminology indicates that the problem is not only a problem of hermeneutics; it is not merely the question of how to interpret and translate the Christian message so that it truly speaks to modern man. As will be seen, the main concern of Bonhoeffer is far beyond the hermeneutical problem; more precisely, the success or failure of interpreting the Christian message and translating it into a meaningful language depends, in Bonhoeffer's view, on a new program of Christian living. But in order to understand what non-religious interpretation of Christianity means for Bonhoeffer, I shall outline his thought on religion and religious interpretation.

From the beginning of his theological career, after he broke with his liberal masters (Harnack, Seeberg, and Holl) and sided with the emerging neo-orthodox movement (primarily Barth), Bonhoeffer never stopped criticizing religion. Liberal Protestantism developed the idea of an "intrinsic capacity" in man to comprehend and receive God. Schleiermacher based his whole theology on man's essential capability "to sense and taste the divine." This was further elaborated upon by Troeltsch and Seeberg, the latter being one of the teachers of Bonhoeffer. Although Seeberg stresses that God transcends human consciousness as Creator and Lord, he contends that

"God can only enter the consciousness as a reality . . . if there is in man an organ for this purpose." Seeberg calls this organ the "religious *a priori*" by which man becomes directly conscious of God. In fact, God and man perform one single simultaneous action in revelation.[22]

For Bonhoeffer, "the religious *a priori*," or any form of an intrinsic capacity postulated in man to receive God, leads inevitably to an idealist metaphysics which eliminates God's transcendence. If God is containable within man, then either this God must be the creation of man, or the human ego which can directly encounter God must be conceived of as intrinsically divine. In either case the logical conclusion is that of an idealist metaphysics where "the inmost identity of the I and God is underlying everything."[23]

Up to this point, Bonhoeffer and Barth agree. Both identify the God of religion with the God of idealist metaphysics and both consider the idealist metaphysics as the most consistent and honest expression of a philosophy of God in general. Consequently, they both insist that the God of religion and the God of philosophy are the highest manifestation of human sinfulness which is man's rebellious attempt (*hubris*) to become God. In Bonhoeffer's view, the greatest merit of Barth is his critique of religion.[24] But he did not carry it far enough, Bonhoeffer insists at the end of his life. For Barth, religiosity is a permanent and essential mark of fallen man. Every man has to go through this stage before the true God of faith passes judgment on him and reunites with himself the fallen religious self of man. To the Bonhoeffer of the *Letters and Papers from Prison,* religion appears as an historical phenomenon of Western culture which is about to disappear to the extent that the world is coming of age.

One can understand now why Bonhoeffer looks with such optimism upon the process of the maturing world. The disappear-

---

[22]See J. A. Phillips, *Christ for Us in the Theology of Bonhoeffer* (New York: Harper & Row, 1967), pp. 59-66.

[23]*Act and Being,* p. 41.

[24]*Letters,* p. 198.

ance of religion is a negative preparation for Christianity. The world becomes more and more godless, but perhaps in its godlessness it is closer now to God than ever before.[25] It is a "promising godlessness," since it gradually eliminates the man-projected conceptions of God.[26] The "non-religious Christianity" is, therefore, not a compromise with our times, a reduction of Christianity to what is still palatable for modern man. Precisely the integrity and the intrinsic nature of Christian faith demands of today's theologian an interpretation which is no longer based on the "religious *a priori*" in man. We will be in a better position to grasp what the new interpretation means if we compare it with the religious interpretation.

The God of religion is a powerful almighty God. But his power is only an intensification of man's power to an infinite degree, and thus, ultimately, his omnipotence is nothing but man's projection. In direct contrast to this idol, the God of the Bible is the crucified and risen Christ. His power is his extreme powerlessness; he becomes Lord of the world through his suffering and death on the cross:

> God allows himself to be edged out of the world and on to the cross. God is weak and powerless in the world, and that is exactly the way, the only way, in which he can be with us and help us. Matthew 8:17 makes it crystal clear that it is not by his omnipotence that Christ helps us, but by his weakness and suffering.[27]

The transcendence of the God of religion is a spurious transcendence. It is only the unlimited extension of the transcendent human subject, a solitary Absolute Supreme Being. (The human subject is defined as transcendent in the philosophy of idealism insofar as his knowledge-creating categories transcend every existing and possible human individual.) The transcend-

---

[25]*Ibid.*, p. 224.
[26]See *Ethics*, pp. 103-104.
[27]*Letters*, pp. 219-220.

ence of the biblical God, Jesus Christ, manifests himself primarily, not in his being in himself and for himself, but in his being freely for man. This total gratuitous love of Jesus Christ for others is his very being. Therefore, the true experience of transcendence is "the experience of Jesus as one whose only concern is for others . . . This freedom from self, maintained to the point of death, is the sole ground of his omnipotence, omniscience and ubiquity."[28]

Religious nostalgia expressed in salvation myths projects a better other-world beyond the grave. That salvation which the religious man seeks is a release from the cares, concerns, and fears of this world. But, in the Christian revelation, everything beyond and above this world exists for this world. "The Christian hope sends a man back to his life on earth in a wholly new way."[29] The Christian will assume total solidarity with his fellowmen, rejoice and suffer with them.

> The religious man abuses God as an ultimate instance to receive help when human perception is (often just from laziness) at an end, or human resources fail: it is really always the *Deus ex machina* they call to their aid, either for the so-called solving of insoluble problems or as support in human failure—always, that is to say, helping out human weakness or on the border of human existence.[30]

So religious man goes to God for help when he is "sore bestead," the Christian "stands by God" when God is "sore bestead." The distinguishing mark of the Christian is the exact opposite of the religious attitude: the Christians "range themselves with God in his suffering."[31] "This is the decisive difference between Christianity and all religions. Man's religiosity makes him look in his distress to the power of God in the world; he uses God as a *Deus ex machina*. The Bible, how-

---

[28]*Ibid.*, p. 237.
[29]*Ibid.*, p. 205.
[30]*Ibid.*, p. 165.
[31]*Ibid.*, pp. 224-225; 222.

ever, directs him to the powerlessness and suffering of God; only a suffering God can help."[32]

The God of religion, as we have seen above, is gradually driven out of all sectors of human life. Religious apologetics desperately try to retain him at least in the sphere of the "personal," "the inner life," of man. Christian psychotherapists and existentialists exploit the secrets of man's inner life in order to show him that when he feels happy, contented, and sane, he is in reality unhappy and desperate.[33] These Christian existentialists insist that "even though there has been a surrender on all secular problems, there still remain the so-called ultimate questions—death, guilt—on which only 'God' can furnish an answer."[34] Bonhoeffer energetically rejects this approach as pointless, since "it looks . . . like an attempt to put a grown-up man back into adolescence" by "thrusting him back into the midst of problems which are in fact not problems for him any more." He rejects it as "religious blackmail, since it exploits man's weakness against his own will." He rejects it as "totally un-Christian, since Christ cannot and should not be relegated to some last secret place."[35] The Bible is concerned, not with the private interior sphere of man, but with the whole man. Bonhoeffer wants Christ to be recognized at the center of man's life: "He must be found at the center of life: in life and not only in death; in health and vigor, and not only in suffering; in activity and not only in sin."[36] So one may say that a religious act is always a *partial* act, activating only a small department of man's life, while the act of faith in Christ is a *total* act, involving the *whole* man.[37]

---

[32]*Ibid.*, p. 220.
[33]*Ibid.*, p. 196.
[34]*Ibid.*, p. 195.
[35]*Ibid.*, p. 214.
[36]*Ibid.*, p. 191.
[37]"Zusammenfassend: wenn 'Religion' einen Zug zum Partiellen hat, können wir statt von 'nichtreligiöser, auch von 'nichtpartieller' Interpretation sprechen oder, wo Bonhoeffer 'weltlich' sagt, von 'das Ganze' Betreffender und beanspruchender Interpretation" (Bethge, *op. cit.*, p. 986).

Finally, religious people consider themselves a privileged class, the assembly of the elect, separated from the sinners. But Christ did precisely the opposite: he had table fellowship with sinners; his whole life was for others, for the world. As leader of an underground seminary, Bonhoeffer held that Christians are called out of the world into the Church in order to become entirely free for the world. In the *Letters and Papers from Prison* the emphasis is more on the second part of the thesis: the Church is Church only insofar as she exists for the world. She betrays her vocation as not only the German Church, but also the Confessing Church of Germany did, when her primary concern is how to assure her survival rather than how to participate in the sufferings of Christ for the world.[38]

This confrontation between the God of religion and the God of faith, between the attitude of religious man and that of the Christian, has shed some light on the problem of the non-religious interpretation of Christianity. We can further clarify it by relating Bonhoeffer's approach to that of the Confessing Church and to that of Bultmann. The merit of the Confessing Church was, as Bonhoeffer sees it, the preservation of "the great concepts of Christian theology" based on the *Church Dogmatics* of Barth. Nevertheless, although her teaching had "elements of genuine prophetic quality" and his worship was authentic, "both remain unexplained and remote, because there is no interpretation of them."[39]

Bultmann rightly felt the need for interpretation, but his solution is false. On the one hand, he did not go far enough; his is still a religious interpretation (God experienced in the inner sphere of the individual person). On the other hand, he went in the wrong direction. Like liberal theology, he attempted to reduce Christianity to its essence and thereby sacrificed its very essence. Bonhoeffer is convinced that "the full content, including the mythological concepts, must be maintained." What

---

[38]See *Letters,* pp. 187-188; 237-240.
[39]*Ibid.,* p. 199.

Bultmann considers as mythology, "the resurrection and so on, is the thing itself, but the concepts must be interpreted in such a way as not to make religion a precondition of faith," just as St. Paul did not regard circumcision as an essential prerequisite for Christian faith.[40]

What is, then, *positively* the non-religious interpretation? There is not much explicit reflection on it in the surviving letters. Every reconstruction of Bonhoeffer's thought will necessarily be sketchy and conjectural. Undoubtedly, it comprises a hermeneutical task. In the "Outline for a Book," he mentions the necessity of revising the creeds (the Apostle's Creed in particular).[41] But, first of all, the nonreligious interpretation is an ethical and spiritual category. The solution of the hermeneutical problem, i.e., understanding, interpreting, and expressing the Christian message in a way which is relevant to the world come of age, depends on the spiritual renewal of the Church. The traditional language of the Church lost its power because the Confessing Church betrayed her vocation by fighting during the Nazi regime for self-preservation as an end in itself rather than caring for the people. Therefore the Church has to remain silent, be purified, and converted. During this period the Church will continue her prayer and sacramental life, but will not proclaim it to the outsiders. In other words, a certain *disciplina arcani* has to be reintroduced. The secret discipline is needed not only because an unrepentant Church cannot proclaim the Gospel authentically; its necessity derives from the very nature of the Christian mysteries. They cannot be imposed on the outsider as "objects" to be learned or memorized. This would be a profanation. The mysteries of faith can be assimilated only in a vital creative process under the guidance of the Holy Spirit. We cannot just proclaim them at any time; we have to wait for "God's own time," which will come with absolute certainty. "Until then the Christian cause will be a hidden and

---

[40]*Ibid.*, pp. 164-168; 199-200.
[41]*Ibid.*, p. 240.

silent affair, but there will be those who pray and do right and wait . . . Christian thinking, speaking and organization must be reborn out of this praying and this action."[42] The *arcanum* is "this praying," the life of faith, praise, petition, thanksgiving, and sacramental fellowship. It must remain hidden for the outsiders, but it should not constitute a separating line between the Church and the world. On the contrary, it is from this center that Christians receive strength and courage to go into the world and live for the world. They accept the sacrifice of silence and of the "incognito" because they trust in the Holy Spirit who will one day bring about the time of a new and powerful proclamation:

> . . . the day will come when men will be called again to utter the word of God with such power as will change and renew the world. It will be a new language, which will horrify men, and yet overwhelm them by its power. It will be the language of a new righteousness and truth, a language which proclaims the peace of God with men and the advent of his kingdom.[43]

Here Bonhoeffer recaptures in a new context a precious tradition of patristic and monastic theology: the relevant and meaningful language of the Christian message is not only the result of an intellectual effort; it is born out of the silent prayer, conversion, and acts of charity of the Christian; the message can be preached only when the time has come, when the Spirit accompanies the action of the preacher in the heart of the believer by making him desire, perceive, and assimilate the Word of God.

One cannot help seeing the plausibility of Bethge's explanation that Bonhoeffer's own life, his acceptance of total solidarity with his nation in the hour of tragedy, when he freely decided to return to Nazi Germany from an American speaking tour, his participation in the plot against Hitler, his taking the

[42]*Ibid.*, p. 188.
[43]*Ibid.*

"incognito" instead of a separate clerical existence, are the best clues to understanding what he meant by non-religious interpretation. He considered his way, not as something extraordinary, but as "the normal way of being a Christian" in that particular situation. His "being for others," as is abundantly clear, was not the expression of a mere this-worldly altruism, but a "participation in the sufferings of Christ" out of which he hoped a new redeemed life would be born.

Of all the radical theologians, W. Hamilton has been most influenced by Bonhoeffer. Yet what he accepts from Bonhoeffer is rather simple, unequivocal, and banal. The dialectic which makes Bonhoeffer's thought at once disturbing and attractive is given up; one of the two poles is dropped, the challenge to further thinking successfully eliminated.

The "world come of age" is no longer a christological, but a sociological concept. It is no longer a penultimate value which calls for the ultimate: redemption and renewal through the cross of Christ. Our maturing world is in itself the ultimate to be valued for its own sake. The dynamic tension between penultimate and ultimate, between human values and God's redemption, between worldly progress and transforming eschatology is dissolved; the latter pole is dropped. Consequently, the optimism of Hamilton is not based on the creating, preserving, and redeeming action of God in Christ, which makes it worthwhile for us to live in this world and hope in its future. His optimism is motivated by a faith in mankind's own power ultimately to solve all its problems or at least to alleviate their burden. It is based on the hope in the success of the "Great Society" and of the civil rights movement. As he himself has put it: "This is not an optimism of grace, but a worldly optimism I am defending."[44]

Hamilton welcomes the process of secularization for its own sake, not because man's growing autonomy discloses the false-

---

[44]William Hamilton, "The New Optimism—from Prufrock to Ringo," *Radical Theology and the Death of God*, p. 169.

hood of the religious conceptions of God and prepares the way for the God of the Bible. He affirms obviously, not only the death of the God of religion, but also the death of the God of Christian faith[45] as the inevitable result of secularization. Therefore, not only the religious interpretation of Christianity, but the very core of Christianity, becomes anachronistic and needs to be discarded. Instead of insisting, as Bonhoeffer does, on the nonreligious interpretation of the *entire* Christian faith, which has to be preserved in its fulness, his problem is to select those fragments of Christianity which, in his view, still make sense for contemporary man. The nonreligious interpretation of Bonhoeffer presupposes a secret sphere guaranteed by the *disciplina arcani* of intense prayer, sacramental life, and fellowship which sustains and animates the struggle of the Christian who lives and suffers *incognito* along with his non-Christian brothers. In the thought of Hamilton, the inner life of the Church is not only to be concealed for the noninitiated; it has simply no meaning whatsoever.

For Hamilton, the only positive task for the Christian in the time of the death of God is to leave the Church and to become a man for others, as Jesus did. To follow a mere man as a final ethical norm (or to uncover Jesus in others if he is only a man) would have been unthinkable for Bonhoeffer. Moreover, in Bonhoeffer's theology, Christ could be totally for others because of his divine transcendence. Divine transcendence, as viewed by Bonhoeffer, means precisely the perfect freedom of total giving. This is the sharp dividing line between God and man. Man can be for others only if, and to the extent that, he participates (it is more than a mere ethical imitation) in the *being* of Christ.

Van Buren does not use the thoughts of Bonhoeffer in *The Secular Meaning of the Gospel*. He merely quotes the famous passage from the *Letters and Papers from Prison*: "Honesty

---

[45]As has been seen above, Hamilton's God of Christian faith is in reality a caricature of the Christian God.

demands that we recognize that we must live in the world as if there were no God. And this is just what we do recognize—before God!" He uses this passage as a strikingly correct description of his own "secular man" for whom the word *God* is dead. But in order to make the text fit his own purpose, van Buren ignores completely the dialectic tension of Bonhoeffer's statement: we are living without God *before God*.

In a later article, however, at a time when he questions all the major conclusions of *The Secular Meaning of the Gospel*, he shows more willingness to examine *both* sides of the paradoxical statement: "living with God without God." He suggests that there may be a close affinity between the world view of William James and that of Bonhoeffer, at least in that of the last stage of Bonhoeffer's career. Van Buren contends that both propose "the hypothesis of a limited God within a pluralistic universe."[46] It is a limited God who works in a "risky, dangerous, adventurous world." He is weak, fails again and again, and counts on the cooperation of man to perfect an unfinished world. The whole enterprise is a gamble; its success depends on the condition "that each several agent does its own 'level best'."[47] It is unnecessary to say how much this rapprochement between Bonhoeffer and W. James is arbitrary. It ignores the very essence of Bonhoeffer's thought: his theology of the cross. The powerlessness of God as revealed in the suffering of Christ is the surest guarantee of his Lordship over the maturing world, and the pledge of the world's final redemption.

J. A. T. Robinson blends Bonhoeffer's ideas of the "world come of age" and of the "religionless interpretation of Christianity" with the "ground of being" of Tillich. Bonhoeffer most probably would have protested against such blending, since he rejects the "religious" interpretation of the dynamics of the de-

---

[46]Paul M. van Buren, "Bonhoeffer's Paradox: Living with God without God," *Theological Explorations*, p. 125.
[47]*Ibid.*, p. 124.

veloping world by Tillich.[48]

Finally, we may ask the question: How could it happen that a man whose faith in the presence of God gave courage and peace to many of his fellow prisoners inspired so decisively a theology without God?

Evidently much has to be attributed to a superficial reading of the *Letters and Papers from Prison*, with no attempt being made to place it in the context of Bonhoeffer's life situation: a man facing death for Christ's sake, experiencing what Christ himself and many martyrs have experienced; the presence of God in the midst of being abandoned by him. Much of this misinterpretation is to be ascribed to reading the *Letters* without the rest of his works. Bonhoeffer never repudiated what he had previously written. On the contrary, there is an inner logic in the direction of his life and of his thinking. Therefore, the last stage is easily misunderstood unless one considers the whole of Bonhoeffer's career and theology.

Yet, even with all these considerations, it must still be admitted that there are in Bonhoeffer's theology inherent ambiguities and deficiencies which can lead one to develop a theology without God.

Let us grant that postulating an active "natural" capacity in man to receive God results ultimately either in a reduction of God to man or in an idolatrous divinization of man, as hap-

---

[48]See *Letters*, pp. 197-198. Harvey Cox is more aware of the complexity and orthodoxy of Bonhoeffer's thought than any one of the above-mentioned group. He uses Bonhoeffer's ideas to a large extent. While discarding the "God of religion," he wants to keep the "God of faith" in a new interpretation. But in spite of his repeated insistence on the utter transcendence of God, he ultimately eliminates the tension between penultimate and ultimate in favor of the former and does not distinguish sufficiently between the maturing world and the coming kingdom, between human effort and final redemption. The transcendent God of the Bible seems to be reduced to the unlimited future horizon of human progress. In this perspective, the Church's only function, as indicated in *The Secular City*, is to be the avant-garde of the forces that build the City of Man. Once again, the Bonhoefferian dialectic between this-worldly involvement and the secret sphere of the Church's life which is the life-giving source of the Christian's secular commitment has been successfully eliminated.

pened in German idealism. But should we for this reason eliminate *any* ability on man's part to know *anything* about God
by reason? If God's *logos* is truly an anti-logos to man's *logos*,
i.e., if the Word is a mere negation and destruction of the human reason, then how can we, in the long run, maintain that
faith in God is not a humanly irrational and irresponsible act?

Granted that it is a perversion of true religion to *use* God
for fulfilling man's need. But authentic Christianity has always considered this an abuse of religion. The basic need of a
truly religious man is to seek and fulfill God's will, not his
own. Yet, once his basic attitude has become that of a child
toward his father, he will always present his daily needs to
God with complete sincerity. He will do it, not in order to
force God, but to express his trust and confidence in Him.

Granted that man can do more today to assure himself
against disease, ill-fortune, and accident. But the basic character of man's finite and precarious existence has not changed.
New and greater dangers come to replace the older ones; just
to mention the most important of all: the total destruction of
human life and civilization has become a real possibility in the
nuclear age. The more civilization progresses, the more the intrinsically finite character of man's development comes to light.
Thus, instead of diminishing, human progress will only increase
man's desire for an infinite fulfillment. Once, however, we de-
clare that there is no need whatsoever in man for God, then, evidently, we imply, however unintentionally, not only the death
of the God of religion, but also the death of the God of Christian faith. If, in his prophetic verdict, Bonhoeffer had distinguished between the false forms of religiosity (individualism, a
morbid cult of inwardness and anxiety, pharisaic separation
from the world, God used as an excuse to avoid human effort
and courage) and true religion, he could not have been so
easily misused by radical theology. It is a source for regret that
Bonhoeffer did not apply his insight concerning the dialectic
tension between the ultimate and penultimate to the relation-

ship between religion and revelation, philosophical knowledge of God and faith in God. At this point he follows even in his latest work the radical Barthian line: the God of faith is the utter destruction of the God of philosophy who is nothing but a human idol. Unlike his attitude toward natural moral goodness, his attitude toward the striving of human reason to know something about God is totally negative.

Another deficiency of his theology that is responsible for a reductionist interpretation is his lack of any Trinitarian doctrine in the last phase of his work. Jesus Christ is simply God made available, "haveable" for man. He is exclusively considered in his relation to us. In fact, this is the structure of his being. Bonhoeffer never mentions the eternal process of the mutual being for each other of the Father and the Son. He does not perceive that Christ can exist entirely for us because he is entirely for the Father. As a consequence, for Bonhoeffer, our participation in the being of Christ is not a share in the intra-trinitarian relationship between Father and Son. It is only a share in Christ's relationship to the world. Therefore, in Bonhoeffer's spirituality, living (and dying) for others is sustained and nourished by the divine transcendent love of Christ for others, but it is not, at the same time, the concrete realization of loving and worshiping the Father, as was the life of Christ. The deepest dimension in the mystery of Christ, his theocentrism (*Theos* meaning God the Father in the language of the New Testament) is conspicuously absent in the final form of Bonhoeffer's christology. No wonder that a Christ whose transcendence is manifested *exclusively* in his being a man for others could be reduced in radical theology to being *merely* a man for others, without any vestige of divine transcendence.

These critical remarks, however, in no way intend to diminish the great values of Bonhoeffer's christology and of his prophetic insights into the nature and the task of the Church. In spite of its deficiencies, the life and the theology of Bonhoeffer most certainly will remain long after the death-of-

God theology will have been forgotten, for his theology is one of the most powerful ferments for a true theological and spiritual renewal in Christianity.

PART FOUR

CONCLUSION

9

EVALUATION AND OUTLOOK

I do not need to treat here all the reactions, Protestant and Catholic, adverse and favorable, to radical theology. Today, about two years after the debate has quieted down, it would not be too useful to examine all the details of the discussion. From the distance of three years, however, we are in a good position to summarize what can be learned from radical theology and to add some reflections which may help avoid a similar dead-end road in the future.

1. The mere exposition of the thought of Hamilton, Altizer, and van Buren, as was done in Part II of this work, has disclosed how shaky and inconsistent their "system" is. Hamilton vacillates between the assertion that God is irreversibly dead and the hope in a new "birth" or "resurrection" of God. God is no longer needed, yet his death is experienced as an "irretrievable loss." Altizer, when cornered, can give only one argument in support of his vision: the life and death of God depend on our faith in him. If we can no longer believe in God, this is the surest sign of his death. And today faith in God is impossible. Yet, he is forced to offer his services to Catholic theology, since his Protestant colleagues cannot be moved away from a biblical faith in a transcendent God. Van Buren himself recently questioned the validity of the major conclusions of his own *The Secular Meaning of the Gospel.*

Besides these inconsistencies, there is one major self-contradiction in all three representatives of the trend: the death-of-God theology has made it crystal-clear that man cannot live without some sort of a god.

In all three "systems" one discovers a certain transfer of the experience of the sacred from what the radical theologians called the Christian god to man. It is the man Jesus, either in the form of the "Great Humanity Divine" (Altizer) or in that of the "neighbor" (Hamilton) or in the model of the "man set free" (van Buren), who takes over the place of the Absolute. The death-of-God theology has brought to light more clearly than any other type of atheism the essentially religious character of every atheistic position. By "religious" character I mean that an atheist, as soon as he engages himself in consistent thinking or acting, must choose, at least implicitly, an Absolute to which he refers everything else and which becomes the ultimate goal of his actions. In Christian atheism, the ultimate value is, evidently, man himself. In fact, nothing else has happened here except that one idol has replaced another: "the man-god" has succeeded "God, the enemy of man." Thus the real choice for man is not between God and no God at all, but between different types of god. The problem, of course, remains: which god to choose. Is there a god who is real and not just the product of man's idol-creating activity? To answer this question is outside the scope of this study. The purpose here is to show the basic inner contradiction which lies at the heart of radical theology.[1]

2. Another important lesson from radical theology is the close connection which exists between the denial of any philosophical knowledge of God (Bultmann, Tillich, Barth, Bonhoeffer, the early Altizer and Hamilton) and the rejection of the transcendent God as theologically irrelevant and existen-

---

[1] Agnosticism seems to be a more widespread phenomenon today than atheism. It succeeds in avoiding a "religious" involvement, but only at the price of giving up any kind of full human commitment.

tially harmful in the death-of-God trend. The elimination of natural theology derived from two sources: from a Kantian skepticism concerning the value of any knowledge that claims to go beyond the boundaries of our empirically observable world, and from the original experience of the Reformers concerning the essential sinfulness of man. The intellect of fallen man has been darkened to the extent that he cannot obtain any true knowledge of God. The essence of sin is man's striving to become god (*hubris*), and his intellect is an efficient accomplice in creating all types of gods. For this twofold reason, only God's revealing action in Jesus Christ can convey a true knowledge of God. But if man is in his very nature completely alien and closed to knowing anything divine, then the knowledge of God through faith can never be man's knowledge. Revelation will then always remain a "stone thrown at him" from the outside, as Barth put it, i.e., an unassimilable foreign body in his universe of different types of knowledge. Such a theological edifice, based on a faith which is only God's act in man and not simultaneously a reasonable and responsible human act, could not have long endured. There had to come a moment when people like Hamilton declared that they could no longer cling to the cliff of bare faith: a faith without any rational foundation had to become irrelevant and humanly unbearable.

Therefore, a re-evaluation of natural theology has become imperative. We have to affirm the possibility of a philosophical knowledge of God, unless we are ready to take the same road which has led from crisis theology to Christian atheism. It is somewhat ironic that at a time when Protestants have come to discover again the importance of natural theology,[2] Catholic thinkers, eager to appear ecumenical and up-to-date, ques-

---

[2]See, e.g., the studies of Schubert M. Ogden, in particular, *The Reality of God* (New York: Harper & Row, 1966); and those of John Macquarrie, in particular, *God-Talk: An Examination of the Language and Logic of Theology* (New York: Harper & Row, 1967).

tion the cognitive value of any philosophical statement about God.[3] If such a position were consistently adopted, the prediction of Altizer would prove true after all: Catholic theology would be reduced to Christology and Christology to anthropology (i.e., God-talk restricted to talk about Christ and the latter to talk about man alone).

Obviously the traditional philosophy of God faces a crisis today. The classic way of finding God through the things of this world has become highly questionable. The outlook of metropolitan man is pragmatic, defined by his technological interests.[4] Nature, and even the nature of man himself, are for him raw materials he intends *to use* in order to transform his own nature and the whole world according to his transformed nature. As a result, the more modern civilization progresses, the more man sees only himself reflected in his environment. The whole world has become, as it were, the mirror of man: wherever he turns, it is his own face, his own works alone, that seem to look back at him. Trapped by his own drive to conquer and dominate the universe, he forgets to see and admire that the universe *is*, that he himself *is*. It is hard for him to realize that man and the universe, that all things of this world, are *given* to be. In other words, he easily forgets to ask the question of being: why do I and things exist rather than not exist?

Since this primordial experience of being has been the starting point and nourishing force of any philosophy of God, the crisis of this experience results in a crisis of the philosophy which arose from the experience. Should we therefore conclude that the growing maturity of man demands that we abandon even the remnants of this experience and its philosophical

---

[3]See, e.g., Eugene Fontinell, "Religious Truth in a Relational and Processive World," *Cross Currents,* Summer, 1967, pp. 283-315.

[4]Such statements, of course, necessarily simplify the issue. What is stated here in general cannot be applied to each individual who lives in a metropolis. See more on this in Hans Urs von Balthasar, *Cordula oder der Ernstfall* (Einsiedeln: Johanes, 1967).

clarifications, in the interest of human development? Or does this crisis reflect a dehumanizing, narrowing tendency in our perspective which must be criticized and corrected, rather than taken for granted as a sign of progress? After all, is it not true that every science, daily life, personal communication, all suppose that there are *beings* and that beings *do* exist? Once, however, the perspective of being is discovered, the God-question necessarily arises and demands an answer. Besides, is it not more and more evident that a one-sidedly utilitarian, exploiting, and mastering approach to the world as potential building material for the City of Man ends up ultimately in destroying the humanness of man himself? The spreading use of hallucinatory drugs, the growing influence of Oriental methods of meditation (like Zen Buddhism) seem to reveal an acute need in today's man to fill the threatening vacuum of an overcivilized artificial life. Van Buren himself, who once described contemporary man as absolutely insensitive to anything specifically religious, has recently revised his stand and admits now the possibility of an irreducible religious experience.[5] Therefore, rather than try to write off religious experience through nature as obsolete, if modern man took some time to "relax" in the full sense of the term, i.e., if he put aside worries about achievement and avoided the temptation to escape into distraction, he would discover a deeper and richer level of human living. Remaining silent, open, and listening, he would perhaps become again attuned to the hidden dimensions of being in and around himself.

3. Our inquiry has also revealed that there is a dialectical connection between the simplistic notion of transcendence in the early Barth, the early Altizer and Hamilton, and the rejection of transcendence in the death-of-God trend. This conception of transcendence has put God and the world in a symmetrical opposition. The creature is in absolute contradiction to God: it is

---

[5]See P. van Buren, "Is Transcendence the Word We Want?" *Theological Explorations,* pp. 169-170.

his exact counterpart. If God is being, the world is non-being; if God is holiness, man is sin; if God is reality, the world is non-reality. The sensitivity of modern man, however, could not endure this oversimplified opposition. In the words of Hamilton:

> . . . we refuse to consent to that traditional interpretation of the world as a shadow-screen of unreality, masking or concealing the eternal which is the only true reality. This refusal is made inevitable by the scientific revolution of the seventeenth century, and it is this refusal that stands as a troublesome shadow between ourselves and the Reformation of the sixteenth. The world of experience is real, and it is necessary and right to be actively engaged in changing its patterns and structures.[6]

Modern man has become so keenly aware of his creativity, of his apparently unlimited potential to exploit, dominate, and perfect the universe that he will necessarily discard a god who contradicts the autonomous reality of himself and his world. If God's reality and the reality of this world are incompatible, then it is evident that today's man will choose the latter.

This contemporary awareness of the autonomous value of our world can help us review and deepen the above-mentioned notion of transcendence in the light of the Christian doctrine of creation and incarnation. If a symmetrical opposition is stated between God and his creation, then God is already captured and defined in our thought categories. As a result, he is then no longer the absolute mystery, but a being reduced to human dimensions. The otherness of God is more mysterious than any dialectical contradiction could explain. Moreover, the true God does not receive his power and glory by diminishing or undermining the autonomy of man. As the older Barth put it: "Only the false gods are envious of man." Only the almighty power of God and his fulness of being can permit created yet autonomous beings to exist distinct from him. They

---

[6]W. Hamilton, "The Death of God Theologies Today," *Radical Theology and the Death of God,* p. 47.

truly are; they have real value; some of them are truly free; yet their autonomy and freedom are real and valuable only because they participate in the perfect reality and freedom of God. We must go a step farther; the more a creature participates in God's being and perfection, the more autonomous his own being is. Man participates in God more perfectly than any infrapersonal creature, created, as he is, unto his image and likeness; therefore he is the only creature in our world who is truly free.

The doctrine of Incarnation can shed even more light on this paradox. The man Christ is, precisely because of his ineffable closeness to God (so close as to become the humanity of the Eternal Son himself), the most truly and fully human being, with whom men of every age, nation, and culture can identify. The Incarnation of Christ, however, was not an end in itself, but aimed at assuming the whole creation into an ineffable union with God. This principle, therefore, must be extended analogously to the whole universe. The universe will unfold its own created perfection; it will be even more itself by being assumed into God's own life than if it had remained in the hypothetical state of "pure nature."[7]

The implications of such an understanding of God's transcendence are far-reaching. In this view, man's increasing domination over nature and his perfecting the universe not only do not contradict God's transcendent power, but they are rooted in the creative and saving act of God. The true value of the de-

---

[7]This paradox cannot be fully understood, but it can be illustrated by a comparison taken from the field of human personal relationships. A mature person never affirms himself to the detriment of his fellowman. On the contrary, a genuine friendship and communion with a mature person will help the other develop himself precisely as *another* person with his unique values and talents. The closer the two friends are to one another, the more they will emerge as unique individuals. This is, however, only a vague and distant image of God's love that makes the creature truly exist as creature by giving and developing the creature's irreplaceable unique reality. See more on this in Karl Rahner, "Current Problems in Christology," *Theological Investigations,* I (Baltimore: Helicon, 1961), 149-200.

veloping world, far from excluding God, presupposes His absolute qualitatively different value as its source, upon which it
constantly draws, and as its final goal, toward which it gradually
approaches.[8]

*   *   *

After this evaluation, I will now offer some reflections which
intend to explain how much the contemporary situation makes
modern man sensitive to the central Christian mystery if that
mystery is presented in an understandable language. This message can truly answer man's deepest aspirations, whereas radical theology, although it was born from the present crisis,
cannot provide a satisfactory solution.

1. The higher contemporary man emerges as master over
nature, with an inexhaustible potential to change further himself and his environment, the deeper sinks his sense of loneli-
ness and insecurity about his own *personal* identity. He is more
aware than ever before of the importance of becoming a "mature person," but he is more worried than ever before whether
or not he *will* become a mature person. The question "who am
I" or "the crisis of identity" seems to bother not just our teen-
agers, but apparently a great number of adults in our society.
It is impossible to list and analyze here all the causes of this
phenomenon. Besides the dazzling possibilities to change man

---

[8]To be sure, no Christian synthesis can be complete without a theology
of the cross. Human progress, too, needs the redemption of Christ. It is
valuable insofar as it is the continuation of, and the participation in, the
creative work of God. Yet, as long as this world lasts, it always remains
open to abuse, and instead of a constantly ascending line, it has its ups
and downs, tragic detours and heroic achievements; the sinful condition
of mankind brands the whole of its history. This is why every new wave
of human effort needs again and again the correcting and purifying mercy
of God. But even the highest and purest accomplishments of human culture and civilization are only a "penultimate" (to use Bonhoeffer's terminology) in God's plan. They are not yet the coming kingdom, though, in
some mysterious way, they condition its coming. Man with all his environment transformed according to his own image and likeness expects still
a final redemption in order to enter fully and definitively into God's own
life.

himself, let me mention only the increasing influence of the modern metropolis on human life. It has broken down the structures of human-size communities. Beyond his own family (if he has time at all to be with them), metropolitan man is forced to relate to an anonymous crowd or, at best, to a purpose-oriented work-team without any deeper human ties. Hence the growing hunger for genuine human relationships, the success of the "T-group" sessions, in which people who worked together for years within the impersonal structure of a business corporation want to learn how to relate to each other in a truly human way. Hence the phenomenal success of Robinson's small book *Honest to God*, which presents God as the depth dimension of human personal relationships. Robinson, however, does not clarify the structure and the implications of such experience. He remains at a half-way point between the Feuerbachian attempt to deify man and a genuine affirmation of God. But, a further analysis of personal relationships in the line of such thinkers as Buber and von Balthasar would prove most helpful in establishing a way to God which is entirely congenial to the sensitivity of modern man.[9] Here I must limit myself to sketching out only a broad outline of what has been said and what I believe could still be said about this approach.

Man today, as has been seen, is searching for a genuine experience of love. Apparently, he does not experience it too often, but he is firmly convinced that it is a *real* possibility. He knows that true love means not only the affirmation and respect of the other person for his own sake, but a readiness for total mutual self-giving. This unconditional love, as a communion between two people affirming and accepting each other's irreducible otherness, cannot be adequately explained without assuming the value-creating absolute love of a personal God. On the one hand, I experience the other self as

---

[9]See, e.g., M. Buber, *I and Thou* (New York: Scribner's, 1958); H. Urs von Balthasar, *The God Question and Modern Man* (New York: Seebury Press, 1967); "Meeting God in Today's World," *Concilium* (New York: Paulist Press, 1965), VI, 23-40.

worthy of an absolute respect, self-giving, and dedication; and I am experienced by the other in the same way. On the other hand, I am also aware, in the same experience, that neither I nor the other are *in ourselves* worthy of such unconditional love. Both of us are finite, imperfect, contingent beings, continuously exposed to the threat of ceasing to exist. Consequently, our own selves cannot give a satisfactory explanation of such esteem and love. In fact, not even a philosophical reasoning which would postulate the creating and preserving love of God the Creator is sufficient. It cannot explain why a *total* and gratuitous giving of one's self to another is truly justified. Only revelation provides us with an answer: it is the *total* self-giving love of God offered to me and my fellow man in Christ that makes us worthy of *total* mutual self-giving.

It is clear that Robinson rightly affirmed that God can be experienced as the ultimate depth of human personal relationship. What he did not see clearly is that only a personal God *above* and *distinct* from the human partners and still intimately bound to them in Christ can be the ultimate ground of such relationships. Only a self-sufficient God, transcendent and radically distinct from his creation, can be the source of *agape*, of that total, unselfish divine love in which a full human experience of love participates.

Von Balthasar seems to be correct, therefore, in assuming that contemporary man faces the challenge of Christianity more directly than did his predecessors. In the past it was easier to confuse the issue of deciding for or against God by hiding behind the God of nature who could be interpreted both as a pantheistic God identical with nature or as a personal God. Today the choice is clear-cut and cannot be covered up. As man painfully but irrevocably emerges above nature as its master, and seeks an answer to explain his own worth and that of his fellowman, he is directly confronted with these alternatives: either to proclaim himself God (as atheistic humanism and Christian atheism did) or to accept the Christian God.[10]

---

[10]See H. Urs von Balthasar, "Meeting God in Today's World."

2. One can confirm the above conclusion by following another path of inquiry. It can be shown—but here I can offer only some brief pointers—that today man is more pressed to face the central Christian mystery of the Trinity than ever before. He is concerned not only about individual personal relationships, but he is forced to draw final conclusions from the inevitable fact that the world, technologically, economically, culturally, and even politically, converges into one. The unity of the world has become today a practical necessity. But, it is also evident that world unity without a genuine world community is more threatening than the previous state of isolation. If enemies are locked up together in a spaceship, the consequences will be more disastrous than if the same enemies were living scattered around a large territory.

All the radical theologians, each in his own way, attempt to develop a community ethics as a starting point for a new humanism. But, they all reject the transcendent God as not only irrelevant to, but actually obstructive of, such ethics. They all conceive of God as a solitary, powerful Lord, in the same line as crisis theology did. They do not even seem to know about the Christian mystery of the Trinity, except in its modalistic distortion, a distortion also inherited from crisis theology. One can at least wonder what would have happened if crisis theology had seen that God is not, as it were, an isolated kingly hermit, but an infinitely powerful and intense communication of life between the Father and the Son in the Spirit. God is such perfect giving and receiving that the Father is Father only insofar as he gives his whole divine life to the Son; the Son is Son only insofar as he gives back everything he received to the Father. And this eternal absolute *process* of communication takes place *in* the Holy Spirit. One can at least ask the question: Is it not the lack of inner personal life, of dynamism and process in their notion of God, that prompted Tillich to conceive of God as the Process of Being, dimming the distinction between God and the world, and that made Altizer adopt a radical form of "process god": God changing into his own opposite, the world?[1]

Again, to learn to live in community is now a matter of life and death for mankind. Either we accept and draw the practical conclusions that man can become truly man only by integrating himself into a community, or else we will not survive as humans. The world has become too small to contain an amorphous mass of self-defensive individuals on its surface. It is at this point that the central Christian mystery speaks to modern man. The Triune God is the model of perfect community that makes us understand why a human person becomes truly himself only if he is integrated into a community. Man is created into the image of the Triune God in whom the most perfect communion (oneness in being) does not only not abolish the distinction of persons, but rather constitutes the personal face-to-face relationship of the Father and the Son in the Holy Spirit.

The Triune God is not only the archetype of every true human community, but, in various degrees and in qualitatively different ways, every human community is a community insofar as it participates in the Trinitarian communion. To explicate, however, all the implications of participating in the Trinitarian life would require another book. The point I am making here is that the central Christian mystery, if presented in the "language" of our times, is perhaps more "relevant" today than ever before. The total self-giving of God to man in Christ that constitutes the infinite value of the human person, the Trinitarian communion as the archetype, source, and ultimate assurance of every human communion, corresponds to the most pressing needs and the secret hopes of modern man.

---

[1]"Process" (*processio*) in the Trinity means an infinitely intense and total communication between the Persons of the Trinity, not *change*, as in contemporary "Process-God" theology.

SELECTED
BIBLIOGRAPHY

I do not intend to enumerate all the books and articles which concern my topic. The purpose of this bibliography is to provide the reader with a selected list of what I consider the most helpful studies *for an introduction* into the problems which I treated in my book. For more detailed research, the reader is advised to consult the bibliography in the footnotes of each chapter.

I. THE *HONEST TO GOD* DEBATE

A)*

1. John A. T. Robinson, *Honest to God* (London: SCM, 1963; Philadelphia: Westminster Press, 1963). This is an ambiguous book, but reveals a great religious sensitivity. It started the discussion on the problem of God. Robinson's two latest books, *The New Reformation?* (Philadelphia: Westminster Press, 1965) and *Explorations into God* (Stanford, Cal.: Stanford University Press, 1967), reaffirm his intention to remain faithful to the Christian God, but do not clear up the ambiguities of his doctrine.

B)

2. *The Honest to God Debate,* edited by David L. Edwards (Philadelphia: Westminster Press, 1963). A collection of the reactions

*A) means primary sources; under B) I have listed studies on primary sources.

137

to *Honest to God*. The best critical studies were written by Daniel Jenkins, David Jenkins, and Herbert McCabe.

3. Eric L. Mascall, *The Secularization of Christianity* (New York: Holt, 1966). The most serious and detailed critique of *Honest to God* and of van Buren's *The Secular Meaning of the Gospel* in terms of the Anglo-Catholic tradition.

II. RADICAL THEOLOGY

A)

4. William Hamilton, *The New Essence of Christianity,* second rev. ed. (New York: Association Press, 1966). It reflects the neo-orthodox position of the early Hamilton. His later radical stand can be understood only against this background.

5. Thomas J. J. Altizer and William Hamilton, *Radical Theology and the Death of God* (Indianapolis: Bobbs Merrill, 1966). This book can be viewed as the manifesto of the death-of-God trend and contains a collection of representative articles by Altizer and Hamilton.

6. William Hamilton, "The Shape of a Radical Theology," *Frontier Theology* (Richmond, Va.: J. Knox, 1967), pp. 69-76. An autobiographical article describing Hamilton's development from neo-orthodoxy to radical theology.

7. Thomas J. J. Altizer, *Oriental Mysticism and Biblical Eschatology* (Philadelphia: Westminster Press, 1961). This book of the neoorthodox Altizer provides the clue for understanding his later death-of-God theology.

8. Thomas J. J. Altizer, *The Gospel of Christian Atheism* (Philadelphia: Westminster Press, 1966). The relatively most systematic presentation of Altizer's death-of-God theology.

9. Paul M. van Buren, *The Secular Meaning of the Gospel* (New York: Macmillan, 1963). A clear, systematic exposition of van Buren's thought.

10. Paul M. van Buren, "Theology in the Context of Culture," *Frontline Theology,* pp. 46-51. In this article van Buren comes closest to the position of an atheistic humanist.

11. Paul M. van Buren, *Theological Explorations* (New York: Macmillan 1968). A collection of articles. Some of them, e.g., "Is Transcendence the Word We Want?" question the major conclusions of his previous book *The Secular Meaning of the Gospel.*

12. Gabriel Vahanian, *The Death of God: The Culture of Our*

Post-Christian Era (New York: Braziller, 1961). Vahanian does not belong to the death-of-God group. In this book he presents a brilliant but one-sided analysis of the idolatrous tendencies in contemporary religious life which ultimately produced radical theology.

B)

13. Albert C. Outler, Schubert M. Ogden, John Deschner, *Trialogue on "The Death of God"* (Dallas: Perkins School of Theology, TM Publications, 1966). A short but thought-provoking panel on the death-of-God trend by three eminent Protestant theologians.

14. Charles N. Bent, *The Death of God Movement* (New York: Paulist Press, 1967). A good summary and evaluation of the theology of Vahanian, van Buren, Hamilton, and Altizer by a Catholic theologian.

15. Thomas W. Ogletree, *The Death of God Controversy* (Nashville: Abingdon Press, 1966). A clear but somewhat uncritical presentation of the thought of Altizer, Hamilton, and van Buren by a Protestant theologian.

16. John Macquarrie, *God and Secularity* (Philadelphia: Westminster, 1967). A popular but valuable introduction into the contemporary problem of God and secularity by one of the best living Protestant theologians.

17. *The Meaning of the Death of God*, edited by Bernard Murchland (New York: Random House, Vintage Books, 1967). A collection of articles dealing with the death-of-God theology. The best articles were written by John Warwick Montgomery and W. Richard Comstock.

18. *The Death of God Debate*, edited by Jackson Lee Ice and John J. Carey (Philadelphia: Westminster Press, 1967). One of the most informative books on the debate.

19. Thomas J. J. Altizer, *Toward a New Christianity: Readings in the Death of God Theology* (New York: Harcourt, Brace & World, 1967). Altizer attempts to find precursors for his radical vision, beginning with Hegel and W. Blake. He presents selected texts with introductory comments.

III. THEOLOGICAL BACKGROUND

A)

20. Rudolf Bultmann, "New Testament and Mythology" *Kerygma and Myth,* edited by Hans Werner Bartsch (New York: Harper

& Row, 1961). This is the famous manifesto of Bultmann's program of demythologization.

21. Rudolf Bultmann, "What Sense Is There to Speak of God?" *Christian Scholar* (Fall, 1960). Man can talk only about the human subject as affected by God's act.

22. Rudolf Bultmann, "Bultmann Replies to His Critics" *Kerygma and Myth,* pp. 191-211.

23. Karl Barth, "An Introductory Essay" to Ludwig Feuerbach, *The Essence of Christianity* (New York: Harper & Row, 1957), pp. x-xxxii. A concise and clear formulation of Barth's theological program in opposition to liberal Protestantism.

24. Karl Barth, *The Epistle to the Romans* (London, New York, Toronto: Oxford University Press, 1953). This commentary, translated from the second revised German edition, had a deep influence on radical theology.

25. Paul Tillich, *The Shaking of the Foundations* (New York: Scribner's, 1948). A collection of Tillich's sermons, one of the sources for *Honest to God.*

26. Paul Tillich, *The Protestant Era* (Chicago: University of Chicago, 1948). To be seriously in the state of doubt means to be in the state of faith. This principle provided Altizer with a "proof" for justifying his death-of-God position.

27. Paul Tillich, *Systematic Theology,* Vols. I, II, and III (Chicago: University of Chicago Press, 1951-1963). In spite of the truly Christian intention of Tillich, a monistic undercurrent is clearly discernible in his system.

28. Dietrich Bonhoeffer, *Ethics* (New York: Macmillan, 1965). It contains the beginnings of Bonhoeffer's new theological vision which will be developed in *Letters and Papers from Prison.*

29. Dietrich Bonhoeffer, *Letters and Papers from Prison* (New York: Macmillan, 1962). Misunderstood and misinterpreted, this book is the most influential source of radical theology.

IV. CONCLUSION

30. Regis Jolivet, *The God of Reason* (New York: Hawthorn, 1958). A popular but valuable introduction into the philosophy of God by a Catholic philosopher and theologian.

31. Jean Daniélou, *God and the Ways of Knowing* (New York: World, 1965). A thought-provoking outline for a contemporary presentation of the mystery of God from different viewpoints: the God of non-Christian religions, the God of Philosophy and the God of Revelation.

32. Hans Urs von Balthasar, *The God Question and Modern Man* (New York: Seebury Press, 1967). It analyzes the causes of contemporary unbelief and shows that the experience of personal encounter is a way to God which is most congenial to the sensitivity of modern man.

33. Hans Urs von Balthasar, "Meeting God in Today's World," *Concilium,* 6 (New York: Paulist Press, 1965):23-40. A more condensed and clearer presentation of the central ideas developed in *The God Question and Modern Man.*

INDEX